The Educated Cat

How to Teach Your Cat to Do Tricks

George Ney with
Susan Sherman Fadem

E. P. DUTTON | NEW YORK

Published in the United States by E. P. Dutton,
a division of NAL Penguin Inc.,
2 Park Avenue, New York, N.Y. 10016.

Published simultaneously in Canada by
Fitzhenry and Whiteside, Limited, Toronto.

Library of Congress Cataloging-in-Publication Data

Ney, George
The educated cat.
Includes index.
1. Cats—Training.   I. Fadem, Susan Sherman.
II. Title.
SF446.6.N49   1987   636.8'0887   87-3058

ISBN: 0-525-24584-7 (cloth)
      0-525-48345-4 (paper)

DESIGNED BY MARK O'CONNOR

10 9 8 7 6 5 4 3 2 1
First Edition

THIS BOOK IS AFFECTIONATELY DEDICATED TO ALL MY CATS.

I've seen a lot of trained animals. But George Ney is one of the few people in the country to have done so much with cats—and with such a large troupe. Without question, he and the cats put on a good show.

When he works with the cats, he is able to pull something out of them that's already there. And his cats seem to have a good time. They get a lot of attention, and they seem to enjoy it all a great deal.

BOB MARTWICK,
animal talent scout
and "valet" to Morris, the 9 Lives Cat

Contents

1 The Cats and I   *1*

2 New Talent for Ney's Performing Cats   25

3 Starting Cat Training   *32*

    The Training Table   34
    Your Cat Should Be Relaxed   36
    Pretraining Contact   37
    How Long Should Training Sessions Last?
       38
    How Old Should My Cat Be for Training?
       40
    Putting Kittens in the Mood for Training
       41
    Stay on the Table!   42
    Getting Used to Noise   42
    Car Travel   43
    Who Should Do the Training?   45
    How Cats Adapt to Newcomers and
       Changes   46
    The Importance of Repetition   49
    Build Logically on Previous Tricks   49

On Days and Off Days   50
If Discipline Is Needed   51
The Importance of Praise   51

4   Building a Repertoire: The First Tricks
    to Teach   53

Sit Down   53
Lie Down   58
Roll Over   60
Play Dead   64
The Death-Defying Trick   68
Beg   69
Shake Hands   72

5   "Presenting in the Center Ring . . ."   75

Jump Through a Hoop   75
Jump over the Baton   78
Cat Chorus   80
Out to Dinner   81
Operator, Please!   84
The Queen and Her Court   86
Strolling Those Babies   86
Tchaikovsky Tomcat   88
Roll out the Barrel   90
Walking on a Leash   93
Personalized Tricks   94

6   Giving Cat Performances for Pleasure
    and Profit   97

Home Performances   97
Senior Citizen Groups   98
Naming Your Show   99

Talking Is Important 99
Avoiding Runaways 99
Getting Publicity 102
Outdoor Performances 103
The Cat-Show Circuit 104
Cat Associations and Clubs 104

7 Making Your Cat Feel at Home 107

Neutering 107
Litter Training 108
Scratching Posts and Houses 109
Give Your Cat an ID Tag 109

INDEX 111

The Educated Cat

1. The Cats and I

There are plenty of dog-saves-man stories. Usually such rescues involve stunning examples of canine loyalty and derring-do. A human trapped in a burning house is yanked to safety by the intrepid family dog. A youngster pinned under a tractor is alive today only because his fearless pooch ran ten miles with a fractured foreleg, then bounded through a glass door to rouse the nearest neighbor.

And where, during such moments of spine-tingling trauma, was the family cat? By reputation, the cat was comfortably asleep on the bed, under the chair, or on the couch.

Well, once and for all, I'd like to set the record straight

on cats. Cats turned my life around and gave me a one-of-a-kind path to a bit of fame, fun, and even some fortune. And I'm not talking about long-maned beasts with king-of-the-jungle dignity in their bearing. I mean those small, notoriously independent-minded, and almost always lovable domesticated cats.

This story, which could do much to establish cats as the genuine heroes of the pet world, begins in Fox River Grove, a wisp of a town in northern Illinois. For years, I had been in the tile and carpet business there. Being something of a natural-born salesman, I was a modest success. Confident that I could do even better, at one time I operated three different stores.

But during the 1970s, disaster struck in the form of the oil shortage. As interest rates went through the roof, the building business was literally falling apart. Contractors were idled. Virtually no one was buying tile or carpet. To say the future was bleak is putting it mildly. Business was horrendous.

Panic-stricken, and with more customer-free moments than I knew how to fill, I began taking the empty, oversize spools discarded by electrical companies and covering them with my ample inventory of unsold plush carpeting. The results I peddled as recreation-room furniture. For ingenuity, the stuff wasn't bad. Every once in a while, I received backhanded compliments. "That would make a good scratching post for my cat," passersby remarked.

After being hit over the head often enough with variations on the same phrase, I got an idea: I would build a line of furniture expressly for cats. Not about to shut the door on any dollars, however, I continued hammering and carpeting the spools, which I touted as end tables for recreation rooms.

Soon, feeling increasingly creative, I became a steady customer at the lumberyard across the street. I would buy strips of plywood, carpet them, and nail them together,

2

Myself with my educated cats Valentine (*left*) and Oscar
(*Courtesy* The Independent Register, *Libertyville, Illinois*)

hoping to strike the fancy of humans and/or their felines.

One day a lady came into the store. I'll never forget her. She wanted an especially nice piece of furniture for her cat. Inspired, I built her a three-tiered scratching post.

It was summertime. The woman's house was on a hill. Alongside the house, when I delivered the scratching post, was a tree limb with branches shooting off in every direction. Instantly, I could visualize turning that limb into something extraordinary for cats. Here was a one-of-a-kind scratching post. All the way home I could barely keep my eyes on the road; I was mesmerized by tree limbs. This was the beginning of my longtime practice of pulling over to the side of the road so I could retrieve the best tree limbs between my home in Mundelein, Illinois, and my store in Fox River Grove.

Somewhat reckless in those days, I frequently made the trip on my Kawasaki 900 motorcycle. With branches strapped like antlers on the back of the seat, I must have looked like some crack marksman after a hunt.

Only my finances were wobbly. Hungry to attract business even before it entered the door, I began displaying cat furniture on the sidewalk. If people thought I was eccentric, that was fine, as long as they thought of me.

My new carpentry technique was straightforward: Take a limb, cut off the branches, then put a carpeted perch or perches on various levels of the limb so the cats can both scratch and jump. The cats seemed pleased. A log, after all, is a cat's natural scratching post, and I believe domesticated cats are attracted to the logs by the odor of the wood.

Again, in the late 1970s, a woman proved a turning point. A female customer flipped over my cat furniture, which had come to include condos, duplexes, ranches, World War I biplanes, spaceships, racing cars, and kitty sofas, chairs, cocktail tables, and floor lamps. I was crazy, she insisted, not to display my things on the cat-show circuit, where a reasonable fee bought a small booth and a captive audience.

For a twenty-five-dollar booth rental, plus gasoline for my battered van, I arrived in Appleton, Wisconsin, loaded down with the forerunners of feline penthouses, an old "Southern plantation," a "gingerbreadlike house," and the Catnip Saloon, all made of carpet scraps, cardboard cores, tree limbs, hollow logs, and wire spools fastened with a pneumatic stapler gun. My wares ranged from $10 scratching boards to color-coordinated, multiunit condos for about $125 per complex. Today some of the fancier versions I continue to make range in price from $20 to as high as $250 apiece.

Showgoers in Appleton were flabbergasted. I sold

4

five scratching posts and houses, which was more than enough to keep me enthusiastic. Even the most indulgent of cat owners had never seen anything like my furniture. Even Morris, the choosy feline of 9 Lives cat food commercials fame, was to become one of my satisfied customers; I made him a three-tiered perch.

Not long after the Wisconsin show, I did the North Shore Cat Club show in Grayslake, Illinois. The crowd was bowled over. I sold out. One woman alone special-ordered four pieces of furniture.

Further inspiration came where I least expected it. From someone else's trash heap, I retrieved a large wooden box. After sawing an opening, I mounted the box on a section of tree limb, added carpet, and presto, there was my first big free-form tree flat. Tickled, I displayed the result in my "showroom": the concrete sidewalk in front of the store.

A passerby from the South Side of Chicago was spellbound. With a deep breath, a prayer, and a lump in my throat, I quoted him a price of seventy-five dollars for the tree flat. He wrote me a check.

Buoyed sky-high by success, I rented space at the Jolly Roger Cat Show, one of the bigger shows in my area. Customers flocked to my booth, although not nearly enough of them to pay my outstanding bills from the tile and carpet business. Despite the thrill of seeing others buy my creations, there were still times when I didn't have two nickels to rub together.

Nonetheless, I tried to look at the positive side. As USA Today would later rave, my kitty condos were "the cat's meow." The Chicago Tribune said I created "the Ritz of cat posts."

Then, in 1980, I did something that took every ounce of guts and blind faith I had. The tile and carpet business had fallen through the floor. I had lost all interest in reviving it. I was bankrupt. So I did what seemed to me the only sane thing—followed my interests and opened in

Mundelein what may well have been the first shop in the country to deal exclusively in cat furniture. Naturally, I called it "Cat House Originals."

"Me-e-e-ow-w-w-w," I would answer the phone, and still do.

People really thought I was crazy. They said I'd never make it.

Most weekends, desperate to attract the largest possible number of buyers, I packed my van with cat furniture and headed for yet another cat show. While the immaculately groomed standouts in the feline world collected their ribbons and trophies, I stayed at my booth, peddling scratching posts and cat houses. Business was respectable. But being a salesman, I knew I needed what stripper Gypsy Rose Lee called a gimmick.

Assistance came from Bonnie Luke, a breeder from Indianapolis. In the fall of 1981, we were both at a cat show in

At a cat show, with four felines playing dead at one time

Hamilton, Ohio. Bonnie walked past my booth with something I had never seen before—a little black Scottish Fold cat. The breed is named for its ears: they fold forward and lie across the top of the head.

These cats originated in the early 1960s. As the story goes, a cat with folded ears was discovered in 1961 in a litter born in Scotland. A little white female, she came into the possession of a veterinarian who bred her with a British shorthair. Scottish Folds, although still fairly rare, are now recognized by the cat fanciers' associations.

Bonnie's cat, a little round-faced male, struck me as so unusual that I completely forgot my own breeding. I laughed uproariously. When I stopped, I knew I had to have the cat. It was absolutely adorable. I imagined putting it on furniture in my shop as an attention-getting prop, like a leggy sex symbol draped across a shiny car hood.

Unfortunately, Bonnie's cat was not available. But months later, she called about another Scottish Fold she said would be even-tempered enough to lounge on one-of-a-kind furniture and to tolerate the hullabaloo at cat shows. Sight unseen, I said I would take it. The price was three hundred dollars.

Mind you, I was envisioning another little black male. Instead Bonnie showed me Tasha, a two-year-old calico-colored female. I was crushed. Had I not been a man of my word, I would have walked out.

Expecting nothing, I placed the cat on a table, prepared to size up my folly. At that moment, as if on cue, the cat rolled over for her tummy to be rubbed. I was smitten. It was love at second sight. I even threw some cat houses into the deal.

In my van, Tasha jumped up on the dashboard. There she rode the entire way home. I was ready to purr.

Previous to this, I had never considered taking a cat on the road to cat shows. With a van full of cat houses and tree limbs, who needed more bother? But a week after

Tasha

acquiring Tasha, I took her and the cat furniture to the Nashville Cat Fanciers show in Tennessee.

Sniffing an opportunity for publicity, I called *The Tennessean* about my custom cat furniture and flop-eared cat. Perhaps the writer I spoke with didn't believe me. Or maybe she mostly did, but still needed convincing. Either way, I wangled an interview.

The next day, a picture of Tasha peering from the window of a cat house covered nearly half the features page of *The Tennessean*. This was to be the first of many newspaper spreads; sometimes we even made the front page.

In Nashville, I also telephoned a local television station. They booked us, too. The combination of Tasha and the furniture was proving irresistible. Moreover, media coverage was helping cat house sales.

Almost every weekend, Tasha and I went to a different cat show. It was during a show in Omaha that we met Tom Drbal of Lincoln, Nebraska, and his remarkable cat, Snoop.

Tom had taught Snoop to jump through a hoop and roll over. I was impressed—amazed was more like it. Like the rest of the world, I'd always assumed that cats were too stubborn and aloof to be taught. I had never seen a house cat that could perform. Like cats to catnip, the Omaha media took to Snoop's tricks and Tasha's looks.

A few weeks later, Tom and Snoop were at the Lincoln State Cat Club show in Chicago. Snoop performed. Still astounded by Tom's accomplishments, I invited him to bring Snoop to Mundelein.

To ballyhoo their visit, I bragged to the boys at Dale's Coffee Shop. "Sure," they said. "Sure, you've seen a performing cat. Now tell us another one." During Tom's stay, confirmed skeptics became confirmed believers. My store was jammed. The whole town wanted to see a trained cat. My own wheels started spinning.

With more confidence than I truly had, I informed Tasha that she would become a performer. "Listen," I said after Snoop left. "You and I are going to learn something." I never did ask Tom about his techniques. In retrospect, I'm sure I didn't want to feel as if I were infringing on his territory. Besides, if and when Tasha succeeded, I was convinced that the country would be big enough for more than one performing cat.

Before Tasha, I had never trained even a dog. As I had no idea where to start, I relied on instinct. Because she lived in my store, where she had no choice but to become accustomed to the noise of the sawing and stapling that went into the making of cat houses, I trained her right on a workbench in the workshop.

As Tasha quickly confirmed, cats have a limited attention span. Lengthy workouts would have been out of the question. She would have been too tired, too bored, or both. Instead, we worked together for maybe five to ten minutes an hour, continuing to do this the next hour and for as many hours as we could squeeze into a day. In addition, Tasha confirmed that cats can be trusted only as far as your arms can reach. During training, I had to be able to touch her. Otherwise, she was all over the shop, everywhere but on her workbench/training table.

Sitting down, which appeared to be the most basic, became trick number one. I put one hand under Tasha's chin and the other over her fanny. How else would you show a cat how to sit? Gently I pushed. Tasha looked at me and wouldn't budge. "Sit, Tasha, sit," I said over and over. I can be stubborn, too.

Never raising my voice, I kept trying. Eventually, "we" tried. And finally, within a couple of days, Tasha was able to sit not only when I tapped her fanny but often when I simply commanded her to.

Was this trick a fluke? Could "we" learn more? From what I knew of dogs, lying down was another standard trick. Again, doing what seemed logical, I put my fingers on Tasha's shoulder blades and pressed gently. She was stubborn. She was reluctant. She was nonplussed and bored. But after three days of practice, Tasha lay down by herself.

I was thrilled. I can't precisely gauge Tasha's reaction. However, she didn't seem to mind the extra praise, petting, and attention. Even during those training sessions when she didn't fully cooperate, I never raised my voice. There's absolutely no point in scaring an animal. Like people, animals respond best to love.

With growing confidence, I introduced another trick:

rolling over. Scratching Tasha's tummy, which I thought might make her squirm and turn, only made her want to be rubbed more. As closely as I could figure, there was no way in the world she was going to roll over when I asked. She needed a reason to roll. For motivation, I supplied morsels of Tasha's favorite treat.

Using my instincts and her growing repertoire, I put Tasha in the lie-down position. Then I moved a treat across her nose (so she could catch the scent) and toward her shoulder. When the treat moved, she turned her head to get it. If the treat was just far enough from her mouth, she had to roll to one side to be rewarded. After a week or so, Tasha went from lying down to rolling to one side and then to the other, all for the same treat.

Whenever customers dropped in, I couldn't resist coaxing Tasha through her routines. People were amazed and amused. If they went home with a cat house, I felt rewarded.

Next Tasha learned to beg, which seems second nature to dogs, but not to cats. For starters, I put her in a sitting position. Then, trying to think like a cat, I assumed she would have to be enticed to lift her front paws. I reached for a treat. To get the treat, Tasha had to lift her body. Every day, I would raise the food a little higher. Finally Tasha went all the way up on her hind legs.

We weren't done yet. Never before had I seen a domesticated cat shake hands. The method I devised was to tap the inside of Tasha's leg softly. For days, her only reaction was to leave the paw in place, or to walk away. But ultimately she became bothered enough by the gentle tapping that she lifted her paw. Then I extended my own hand to shake. We did.

Within six weeks, Tasha had learned all five of these tricks. I was on cloud nine. Still, there was something I was dying to know. Would Tasha perform only amid the usual noise and activity of my shop, or could she entertain elsewhere?

In search of a receptive, but preferably not too critical, crowd, I volunteered to put on a demonstration at the Brentwood North Nursing and Rehabilitation Center in nearby Riverwoods, Illinois. If all else failed, I figured the seniors might enjoy seeing a new breed of cat. To Tasha's everlasting credit, she was a howling success. She did everything. She sat down, lay down, rolled over, begged, and shook hands. Naturally, there were times when I had to coax and recoax her. Sometimes she'd balk at directions and give every indication of not cooperating. But then, to the crowd's delight, she'd execute the trick.

I did my share of performing, too. Because the full sequence of Tasha's tricks, even with her unrehearsed stalling, took only minutes to complete, I ad-libbed. And ad-libbed. And ad-libbed. But it was a day when we could do no wrong. The senior citizens gave us our start. They were our first official audience. Tasha and I have returned to the Riverwoods center many times.

By the fall of 1982, I had a minor celebrity on my hands. Tasha had graduated from my workbench to stages and platforms at cat shows. And wherever I took her and the cat furniture, her performances generated newspaper and television coverage, which in turn helped draw crowds to the shows and to the cat furniture at my booth.

Kansas City will always be special to me. At a cat show there, a young woman bird-dogging for a photographer asked if Tasha could pose, for fifteen dollars, for Hallmark greeting cards. Does a pig wallow in the mud? Just show us the way, I fairly shouted.

The photographer, who had worked, or tried to work, with numerous animals, wanted Tasha on the table. "No problem," I said nonchalantly.

"Tasha, will you please sit down," I said. Immediately, she bent all four legs and dropped down on the table. The photographer's mouth opened so wide the cat might have jumped through.

A Cat Combo

"I don't believe it!" he exclaimed. He worked with Tasha at least a half hour. His young assistant called the session "one of the most fascinating we've ever had." Tasha's photos remain on file with Hallmark. The last time I checked, a company spokesman said there was "always a chance" she would pop up on a card, poster, or jigsaw puzzle.

Meanwhile, Tasha's repertoire grew. In time, I had her up to eighteen tricks, including jumping through a hoop, playing a toy piano (surprisingly, the trick was not in the playing, but in getting her used to the noise), rolling a barrel, riding in a baby stroller, and sitting in one of my homemade carpet-covered high chairs.

But believe me, I'm no genius at in-depth communication with animals. My secret, and it's really no secret, is to think of a possible trick, break it down into steps, and practice with the cat, at the cat's pace. Furthermore, I never got angry with Tasha.

As long as I've known her, Tasha has always been something of a little grandma. She has three speeds: slow, slow, and slow. But I don't hold it against her. When you love an animal, you love it. I've always believed you can tell a lot about people by the way they treat their pets.

Tasha was far from just a backdrop for my cat furniture. From Al Hall, executive producer of WGN-TV's "Bozo Show" in Chicago, she got her first nationwide exposure. In 1982, after a couple of phone calls from me— Ney, my last name, is pronounced like "not shy"—and the delivery of a few stacks of Tasha's newspaper clippings, Al booked her for a guest appearance. The show, starring a costumed clown, is picked up by stations across the country. Tasha and I appeared the same day as some actors who danced with flags.

Tasha didn't have to dance. She charmed the kids in the studio by sitting on command, sitting in her custom high chair, rolling over, and playing dead.

*   *   *

Although preparing for the show had been all I could think about, on the way there I managed to acquire the cat that was to become Tasha's performing partner. Presuming that anyone with a cat furniture store had to be wild about cats, a plaintive-sounding woman called on the phone. She was moving to a new apartment where cats were not allowed. So please, please, wouldn't I take her cat?

"Honey, I already have a cat," I tried to explain. "I'm not interested in another one." But she was insistent. The cat was only six months old. It was a nice cat, she said.

"Well, bring her by," I consented. But I made no guarantees. Certainly, I could find a reason why the cat would not fit in at the shop or on the road.

Just as my business associate, Ed Zerr, and I were walking out the back door with Tasha, heading for the "Bozo Show," the woman arrived. Her cat, a little short-haired orange-and-white tabby, was a garden-variety "purr alley."

The soon-to-be former owner dumped her in my arms. The cat hissed. I put her on the workbench. She hissed again and spit, like tacking an exclamation point onto a sentence. But what sold me is that when I put her in a sitting position on her haunches, she stayed seated. Meanwhile, she looked at me and hissed.

Right after the "Bozo Show," I started playing with Miss Hiss, or The Hisser. What else could I call her? She didn't scratch and she didn't bite, but she sure could hiss. It was absolutely awful.

On and off for a couple of days, I continued to pet and hold her. A fondness for handling, I concluded, is a first step toward training.

Uncertain that I would have any luck whatsoever, I began using Tasha's training techniques. I'm not one to walk away from a challenge, but I wasn't expecting much.

If ever a cat seemed unteachable, it was Miss Hiss. The Hisser is outspoken, aggressive, and ready to pick a fight. If you've got any sense, she's not the kind of cat you go up to and pet. Affection, to her, is a soft hiss.

To this day, Miss Hiss merely tolerates me. After all, I feed her, give her heat in winter and air conditioning in summer. But of all the cats I've had, going back to when I was a kid in St. Louis, Michigan, it would be very, very difficult to find a cat I love more than The Hisser. She's like the black sheep of the family. Some of us feel closest to the ones that give us the most problems.

And I never expected The Hisser to be trainable. We started with "sit down," and went to "lie down" and "roll over." When Miss Hiss declined to initiate a behavior herself, I kept her interest with the promise of treats. She earned them. Overall, she was easier to train than Tasha. She was younger—but then, I also knew more about what I was doing. After three weeks, Miss Hiss had learned ten tricks. She retained her hiss.

What I gained was the hope, which later became a belief, that virtually any cat that can be held can be taught something.

Today The Hisser stars in a routine I've dubbed "The Queen and Her Court." Befitting her somewhat untouchable status, she sits elevated on her own little throne, amid her courtiers. She also has learned to jump barricades and engage in the somewhat unroyal behavior of begging.

For one of her maneuvers, "The Death-Defying Trick," Miss Hiss was singled out for praise by cat magazines and many major newspapers. On her back on a carpeted two-by-four balanced on two benches several feet above the ground, she remains "as immobile as an Indian fakir on a bed of nails," chronicled *Cat Fancy* magazine. Then I snap my fingers, and she twists, drops, and scampers off.

Shortly after Miss Hiss joined the act, the Hyatt Regency Hotel at Crown Center in Kansas City reopened after being closed for reconstruction work. Apparently because Tasha had made such an impression during her previous trip to the city, a promotional group invited her to be among performers at a gala rededication of the hotel. Miss Hiss came along for the ride.

This was their first double-billed commercial venture. We did several shows, spread over two days. And would you believe, Miss Hiss—playing dead—got her picture on the front page of the *Kansas City Star?* In the cutline, she was mistakenly identified as Tasha. I was too excited to quibble.

Besides, Miss Hiss's and Tasha's growing fame was keeping my mind off personal woes. I was having fun, but I was still strapped for cash. To buy gasoline for the 560-mile trip from Mundelein to Kansas City, I sold some cat houses. When I learned that payment for the cats' performances would be mailed to me, I couldn't pay for a motel room. Instead, I slept with the cats in the van, on the motel's parking lot.

But I couldn't feel down for long. Every awestruck newspaper story and TV spot about my "all-star cats" and their mostly "purr-fect" performances generated more headlines and press coverage and more attention. We made *The Washington Post*, the *Dallas Morning News*, and *The Toledo Blade*. United Press International sent a feature on our show over its wires nationwide.

Soon the cats and I were doing shows from the Ramada Inn in Albuquerque, New Mexico, to the Holiday Inn in Louisville, Kentucky, the Teamsters Hall in Cedar Rapids, Iowa, and the Thomas Jefferson Community Center in Arlington, Virginia. At the Cow Palace in San Francisco, we must have performed before a total of twenty thousand people in two days.

And observing that my four-legged performers were five-star celebrities, Animal Consultants of Joppa, Maryland, a company that organizes cat shows, signed me as an "advance man." The agreement was that if shows paid the booth rental fee for my cat furniture and paid for my lodgings, I would arrive a day early in their city, where my cats would invariably garner media attention, and the kind of publicity that helped increase audiences for the upcoming show. One of the first shows I did on this basis was held at the Hilton hotel in King of Prussia, Pennsylvania.

Sometimes I had to pinch myself to make sure I wasn't dreaming. Here I was, that "crazy" guy who believed there was a future in cats!

In business, as I learned a long time ago, you never know when your breaks will come. One day in Mundelein, a truck driver came into my store to make a delivery. Because showing off the cats had become part of my routine, I had the cats roll over, jump through a hoop, and do a few more tricks. Dave Forgue, the driver, opened his eyes wide. He seemed amazed. Dave's wife, Joan, was the emcee of a game show on cable TV. He said he was so impressed that he said he would mention the cats to a friend of his, a TV cameraman.

If I held my breath every time someone promised to help steer the cats' careers, I'd have turned blue a long time ago. Instead, I try my darndest not to get my hopes up.

But, sure enough, the cameraman, Reno Minorini, did call. He wanted to do a whole show on the cats. I was thrilled. We set a date.

Then, just before the filming in 1984, Reno, who has since died, telephoned. Something had come up. Oh, well, I thought, ours was not the first show to be canceled. But lo and behold, a few hours later Reno called back, a crew from Capital Cities Cable came to my store, and they did a half hour on the cats. Mark Hodges was the producer.

Afterward, Reno asked me to come to a studio in nearby Highwood, Illinois. With Tasha as the hostess, I was to be the host of a new public-access program for Capital Cities Cable. We called the show "All About Animals."

Even Marlin Perkins, whose then-assistant on "Wild Kingdom," Jim Fowler, would later perform on the same stage as my cats in New Mexico, had to start somewhere. I was game. For my first program, I invited the mayor of Highwood. "Your Honor, forget about politics," I told him. "Just bring your dog."

He did. Over the years, magicians brought their turtledoves to appear on "All About Animals." A sandwich-shop owner and country-western singer brought dogs.

My cats also made appearances. The troupe was expanding. Madame Tanya—every cat house needs a madame—joined Tasha and Miss Hiss in 1983. The Madame, a bright-eyed, classic brown tabby, was four months old when Bonnie Luke brought her to me at a cat show in St. Louis. I paid $250 for her. Like Tasha, she is a Scottish Fold.

I got Madame on a Saturday morning. When we left the show Sunday afternoon, she was doing three tricks. I trained her in between selling cat houses.

Madame's biggest crowd-pleaser, which was also one of the easiest tricks to teach, was jumping through a hoop. Supremely confident of her ability and mine, I held out a little bit of food, inducing her to jump a short distance from one piece of my furniture to another. Then I added a wire coat hanger, which I bent into a hoop. I put Madame on one side, the food on the other, and the hanger between them. Seeing and smelling the food, Madame walked through the hoop. Knowing we were on the right track, I moved the food back and raised the hoop slightly. The Madame soared. A woman standing at my booth at the time gasped. Crowds think nothing of it when circus lions jump through hoops. But house cats?

The Madame was not to be the last of my acquisitions. It's funny, but except for Tasha, I rarely go looking for cats. Invariably, they come to me. One such procurement began quite unexpectedly in 1983. A friend of mine, Susan Hochstadter, and her daughters, Karen and Elizabeth, had accompanied me to a show I was doing for senior citizens in Glen Ellyn, Illinois. Working with three cats, I needed all the extra hands I could get.

Earlier, the Hochstadters had taken one of their cats to Dr. Petro Popowycz, a veterinarian and owner of the West-Side Animal Hospital in Chicago. In his office, they spotted a little orange-and-white mixed-breed cat. "George," the girls pleaded after the show, "you've just got to see it."

I had been through this before. "I don't need another cat. I already have three," I insisted. But strictly to pacify the girls, or so I thought, I drove to Chicago.

She turned out to be a young cat perhaps twelve weeks old, with a tail three times as long as her body and the biggest mouth I had ever seen on a kitten. On the examination table at the vet's office, she walked from one end to the other, yowling. She sounded as if she were demanding that I take her home. I obliged.

It was Valentine's Day. I named her Valentine.

Three days later, when I did a videotape program, "How to Train Your Cat," Valentine was one of the principal stars. She had learned eight tricks. Although she was all cat, with at least part of her mind perpetually on mischief, she was a quick, if sometimes unruly, study.

To this day, Valentine is the friskiest member of the troupe. I can be working with her on a table when, all of a sudden, she's out in the crowd. The audience loves it. "Now, if you see her, just reach down and bring her back up," I always say. "She's a calm and loving cat." One of her loves just happens to be trouble.

One of her more commendable maneuvers is what I call "Cat-a-Back." First, Valentine plays dead. To accomplish this, I kept turning her on her back, softly reassuring her, rubbing her tummy, and praising her. Then to embellish the trick, I began slamming my hand down near her. In time, Valentine didn't flinch.

My own emotions were not always so easily contained. From my next Scottish Fold from Bonnie Luke, I got a strong dose of sadness. I paid $250 for the cat, intending to sell it to a customer of mine. But for reasons I have never understood, the customer detested the cat. Rather than risk further unhappiness, I kept the cat. He was an easygoing golden brown tabby. I named him Peanut Butter. He was about five months old.

Peanut Butter was a natural. Within a few days, he learned to sit in a chair, sit down, and jump through a hoop. One day I was driving him to a cat show when I had to make a stop. I locked the van.

When I returned, Peanut Butter was gone. The only thing I could think of was that he might have escaped earlier when I paid a toll at a toll booth. Perhaps, when the window was still down, I had turned my head a second and not seen him jump out.

I'll never know. But I was devastated. It doesn't take long to develop love for an animal. Peanut Butter and I were together just a few months. Thinking he might have climbed a tree, I called the fire station. I placed ads in the newspaper. But I never heard a thing. And one of the saddest parts was if anybody ever found him, I'm sure they never knew what a talented animal they had.

With Oscar, my next cat, I knew from the start. I was doing a cat show in Arlington, Virginia, in 1984 when I walked past a booth set up by the Humane Society. I walked by once on the way to my own booth of cat furniture and then, for some reason, turned around. That's when I spied Oscar. He was orange and as "purr alley" as they come. I picked him up. Needless to say, he became mine.

Oscar was about eight weeks old. I adopted him on a Saturday night. Unbelievable as it may sound, and there were plenty of people in the exhibition center to vouch for it, Oscar was doing ten tricks by the time we left Sunday evening. He never mastered another stunt after that, but that's the way some cats are.

Besides sitting down, lying down, rolling over, and playing dead, Oscar could jump through a hoop, ride in a baby stroller, and eat in a high chair. At the tender age of eight weeks, he fitted right into the act with the other cats. He was a pro.

I now had the largest performing cat troupe in the country. In truth, I had almost no competition. Tom in Omaha had one trained cat. I'd heard about a man on the West Coast who did some work with cats. But, presumably due to what seems like cats' standoffish natures, most people never teach a cat a single trick, let alone five or ten. Between my four cats, we had forty tricks.

Billed as "George Ney and His Performing Cats," we entertained at a shopping mall in North Olmsted, Ohio, where actress and pet lover Betty White was also on the program. We've played convention halls, armories, exhibition centers, nursing homes, schools, and at Boy Scout dinners and benefits for heart transplant recipients.

Since 1982, when I first took Tasha and the furniture to a cat show, the cats and I have been on the road an average of thirty-five weekends a year, traveling forty thousand miles annually. Already, I've worn out three vans.

Meanwhile, many of the cats have become stars in their own right. Tasha was my first pinup girl. In 1985 she was selected promotion cat for the American Veterinary Medical Association's National Pet Week. Outfitted in director's togs, she and a dog made a tape for public television. The cats were also featured in *Cats*, *Cat Fancy*, and *The Cat Fancy Almanac* magazines. In Green Bay, Wisconsin, Oscar did a Chevrolet commercial with legendary football star Dick Butkus, formerly of the Chicago Bears. The TV commercial was something of an inside joke.

Earlier, retired linebacker Ray Ninske of the Green Bay Packers had done an Oldsmobile commercial with a dog he called Butkus. Now two-legged Butkus was getting

22

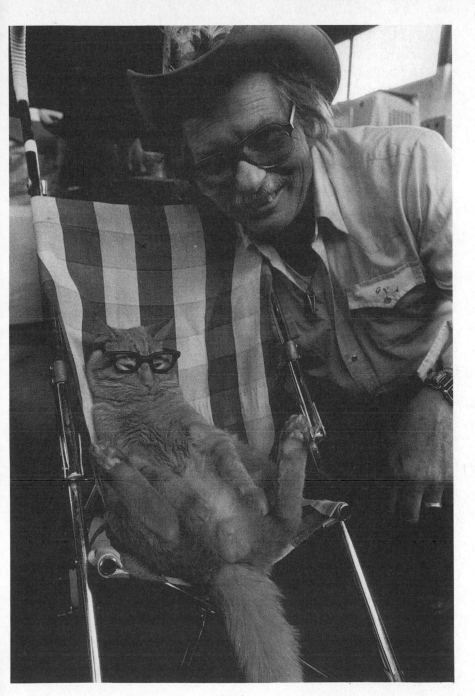

Oscar

even. During the filming, Oscar was known as "Ninske." Like his namesake, he wore a pair of horn-rimmed glasses. Bespectacled Oscar—I mean, Ninske—sat behind the wheel.

Later Oscar made a guest appearance on "Lady Blue," a short-lived detective series on ABC-TV. With commendable aplomb, he played a cat held hostage, a gun to his head.

Oscar was my "strong, silent type," my he-man. All that made losing him all the harder. On our way to a cat show in East Brunswick, New Jersey, in 1986, I stopped at a restaurant in Du Bois, Pennsylvania, and at a truck stop in Milton, Pennsylvania. At one or the other of these stops, Oscar vanished.

Thinking back, he had to have been taken from my van. Otherwise, I just can't imagine how he got out. And after the nightmare with Peanut Butter, I couldn't have been more careful.

I was heartsick. I drove back two thousand miles, retracing my steps and trying to find him. I'd had Oscar for eighteen months. I'd raised him since he was a kitten. Grief-stricken, I took out newspaper ads. Stories about Oscar, the famous cat, appeared in several Pennsylvania towns. I contacted city officials. Someone in Milton said Oscar had been found. I drove back to Milton. To my sorrow, it was the wrong cat. In Du Bois, a group of retarded children helped so much in the search that I gave a benefit in their honor; the other cats performed.

The police looked for Oscar, animal wardens were alerted, everyone bent over backward to help. It's unbelievable what people will do during a crisis. But we never found Oscar. I have the memories, the newspaper clippings, and adorable, studious-looking photos of Oscar in horn-rimmed glasses, held by a rubber band around his head. But I never saw Oscar again.

There will never be another cat like him.

2. New Talent for Ney's Performing Cats

For a while, I didn't think I could ever become so attached to another cat. But not long before Oscar left, I had found Scupa. As usual, I didn't plan the acquisition. I was cat-sitting for my daughter, Cheryl, when her cat, Misty, had kittens. The cutest was a champagne-colored one. From day one, I would pet him. By the time he was five weeks old, and still too young to be separated permanently from his mother, I started working with him in my hands, then putting him back at her side. I had never started a training program with so young a kitten. But of all the cats I've had, this one without question is the most unusual. He's so bright, so playful, obedient, intelligent, and receptive, and such a fast learner.

To name this little one, I adapted something from Cowboy Bob, a friend of mine who periodically has an early-morning children's show on Channel 4, WTTV, in Indianapolis. Bob, who likes to scuba dive, named his dog Scuba, which he says stands for "self-contained underwater barking apparatus." Since a cat has a purring apparatus, I have a Scupa.

And through it all, he's a classic little bad boy. He's into everything. You try to write, he's on the desk. You build cat furniture, he jumps up on a perch, ready to give instructions. He drives you crazy. All he wants is to be petted. If customers in my shop don't give him enough attention, he jumps up on the counter and reaches over, pawing their shoulders or their hair. You've got to love him.

These days, Scupa shares the stage with bluish-colored Victoria. To look at her, you'd think she was a blue-blooded Russian blue. I haven't found a soul to vouch for her ancestry. Most likely she's a mixed breed. But whatever, she's a terrific cat. Again, I had virtually nothing to do with acquiring her. I happened to know Charlene Whitney, a dog trainer who keeps the books at Cat House Originals, which I've now relocated to Wauconda, Illinois. Charlene also finds owners for homeless pets. She can spot a softy a mile away.

"Oh, George, you've just got to see this cat," she pleaded one day.

"Sure, sure," I said. Well, one Saturday she brought in one of the most pathetic little kittens I have ever seen. The cat looked so sick I didn't think she had a chance. A vet diagnosed intestinal problems. I questioned whether it was fair to make the kitten endure such pain.

But fortunately, I was spared all life-and-death decisions when the vet volunteered to keep her a few days, then sent her home with medicine. Still, I saw no improvement. For a while, it was touch and go. It took several more days before I became convinced that she was going

Out for a stroll

(Photo courtesy of Pioneer Press, Inc., Mundelein, Illinois)

to make it. Although a long way from being robust, Victoria—as I called her—was a charmer. As she became stronger, I began training her.

Like Scupa, Victoria now "answers" the telephone. She also jumps over a baton and eats in a high chair. And considering all she had gone through earlier, her public debut was particularly grand—being wheeled down Fifth Avenue in New York in a baby stroller (I was in town for the Empire State Cat Club show).

Not about to be outdone, Scupa was tapped by talent scouts to play a youngish Garfield. The story line, in a TV commercial, featured a youngster playing cartoonist Jim Davis, Garfield's creator. Young Jim, who lived on a farm, lost his cat. The pet, ably played by Scupa, was discovered in the hayloft. Showing more patience than some humans, Scupa posed in the hay one entire afternoon.

Our troupe is still growing. Once again, I have Charlene to blame/thank. She and her husband were scheduled to take a trip. The day before, she received a frantic call about five kittens. Unless homes were found, the kittens would be put to sleep. And, God love her, Charlene was ready to give up her trip to care for those kittens. I couldn't have that on my conscience.

Pretending to have things under control, I located a potential surrogate mother—a cat whose own kittens had just been given away. Initially, the mother cat would have nothing to do with the strange kittens. But mercifully, she changed her mind.

Eight weeks later, I brought the five kittens to my store. For four of them, I found homes; the fifth I kept. It was Halloween. I called the kitten Spooker.

He has a black face. Except for a black stripe around his body, the rest of him is a smoky gray. His first day at the store, I started his training program. At the age of ten weeks, he did his first public performance at the Rush Presbyterian St. Luke's Hospital in Chicago. The kids loved him.

He also went along with the other cats to shows on Staten Island, New York, and in Danbury, Connecticut. It was at the Hilton Inn, Danbury, that the cats and I got an extra surprise on my sixty-second birthday. To my astonishment, the maître d' and the manager of the American Cat Fanciers' Association show wheeled in a birthday cake. Although it was blazing with just a handful of candles, there was still smoke enough when I blew them out to set off the hotel's smoke detector. You can imagine all the yelping, screeching, and howling—from both two-legged and four-legged guests—in the exhibition hall. Before the cats were pacified by their owners, who quickly learned the source of the pseudo-bonfire, some of the felines were ready to go through the roof. But not my troupe. Accustomed to noise and crowds, they merely perked up their ears.

I think the show that worried me the most was one I had to do without my regular cats. The performance at the University of Southern Maine in Portland could well have been a disaster. Motor trouble sidelined my van before I ever left Mundelein. Calculating what it would have cost to fly with all the cats, plus assorted cat furniture, to Portland, I was into next year's earnings. Instead, hating to break a date—especially one I was to be paid for—I attempted my own logic-defying feat. I flew alone, arriving empty-handed, but with one request: Please, ask the TV crew filming me to bring along a cat, preferably one that can be held.

Talk about panic. If ever my performance was going to bomb, this was it. I could see it now. I would be supplied a cat that would do absolutely nothing. No matter what I did, it would still do nothing. Making a bigger fool of myself by the moment, I would ad-lib and ad-lib until, finally, someone would have to cart me off. There would go my bookings and my future. I would be a laughingstock. "Crazy George Ney, I told you so," they would cluck back home.

When one of the TV station's employees handed me his outdoor cat, I was hardly reassured. While the crew set up in my hotel room, where the segment was to be filmed, I had maybe fifteen minutes with that animal. "That's a good cat. That's a good cat," I kept saying, praying the message would sink in. I never stopped working with the cat, petting him, sweet-talking him, coaxing him to sit, roll over, and play dead.

The cat ran under the bed. The cameras were rolling. Here was my moment of truth. I scooped up the cat. And, knocking the socks off even me, I had him doing three tricks. He sat, rolled over, and played dead. And all along I'd thought I would be the dead duck.

That's the thing about cats. They never cease to amaze . They're smart—smart enough to have bamboozled most of us into thinking they can't be trained. Back into antiquity, cats have been revered. Because their eyes glowed at night, it was thought they reflected the light of the sun-god, Ra, who worked against evil.

Egyptians elevated cats to the rank of deity. Out of fear, owners catered to their every whim. When cats died, the Egyptians had them mummified, along with embalmed rats and mice for munching in the hereafter.

However, through the ages, virtually no one thought to train a cat to do tricks. That's why, even in a high-tech age of infinite possibility, performing cats continue to amaze. No matter how many times I crisscross the country, people still refuse at first to believe what my cats can do. Until they've seen us perform, the cat lovers don't believe it. And priding themselves on skepticism, neither do the media people. This attitude changes quickly when I walk into a metropolitan newspaper office. Even among hard-boiled reporters, "George Ney and His Performing Cats"—for convenience, I usually travel with no more than three at a time—can raise a real ruckus.

I wheel in the cats in a baby stroller. Reporters, seemingly chained to their word processors, look up, even when they're on deadline. By the time Miss Hiss rolls over, Victoria jumps through a hoop, and Valentine plays dead, all work has stopped. About that time, the managing editor storms out, demanding to know what's monopolizing his staff.

In the next day's paper, pictures of the cats generally occupy all the space that unwritten stories might have filled.

Nonetheless, cats will be cats.

Take the Madame. As many tricks as she knows, one of her favorites, which is completely self-taught, is hiding from me before a show. Some days I've spent an hour looking for her. Since the Madame turned six years old, I have mostly retired her from the performance circuit. Tasha, too, went into semiretirement at the same age, though she is still among the stars in my new cat-training videocassette.

The Madame has also found a new outlet. During her first cat show competition, in Wheaton, Illinois, she was named a grand champion. She brought home four ribbons and two rosettes.

I dearly love my cats. And it's the training, by the methods I'm about to explain, that has added most to my enjoyment. Not that you don't love a cat for just sharing your living space. But when you take the time to teach that animal something, and it responds, a special bond develops.

Remember the last time you taught a child to whack a baseball, or perhaps gave a teen-ager driving lessons. Now imagine giving your cat a command, or coaxing it with the promise of a reward, and seeing it obey perfectly. Or showing off your pet in a program of entertaining tricks before an audience of enthusiastic, applauding spectators. That's a thrill not to be missed. And your feline, I'm convinced, will be all the richer for it. Cats derive pleasure from performing, too.

3. Starting Cat Training

*C*ontrary to popular belief, there is plenty of ham in cats. After training the nation's largest multiple-cat performing act, I'm sure of it.

Whether your dream stage is your living room or one of the country's exhibition halls, cats can really ham it up. At cat shows, some of my cats absolutely cannot wait to get up in front of an audience. When they do, they roll over. They play dead. And this is all at their own instigation.

What I do at such moments is stand back with my arms poised, if necessary, to engulf the cats. These are not rock stars. My fear is not that the headliners will be mobbed, but that they will jump off the table and dart into the mob or, worse yet, make unescorted getaways from the exhibition hall.

Cats, even performing cats, are like that. You just accept it. In fact, such catlike conduct adds to the public impact of the training techniques you are about to learn.

But first, some things must be unlearned. Previous mind-sets about felines have to be discarded. Consider the dog. People who acquire dogs expect to teach them things. Whoever heard of a Rover, in a household for any length of time, that didn't learn to roll over or to get up on its hind legs and plant a kiss on someone's cheek?

Yet with cats, owing to prior human conditioning and the mistaken notion that cats are utterly independent and intractable, most humans attempt no teaching at all.

Even with Tasha, the cat I eventually taught eighteen tricks, I at first desired nothing more than an animal, albeit an attractive one, to sleep on my cat furniture and thereby draw attention to it.

Most of us have been perfectly content to have cats nuzzle against our ankles and snooze in our laps, invariably when we try to watch TV or read. Such pleasures are not insignificant. I don't advocate giving them up.

However, what Tasha and the others have taught me is that training adds immeasurably to your devotion to the animal. You are never closer to a cat than to the cat you train. After all, you've shared something. You've worked together. And all the while, you praised the cat. You let it know that you truly love it.

For cats as well as humans, there are dividends. When an animal is trained with love, it typically becomes more gentle and loving. I can see it with Miss Hiss. While *sweet* is a word I'm still hard pressed to use in describing her, even The Hisser has softened since she began performing. Now she hisses a little less.

But don't get me wrong. Cats will never be trained to the same extent as dogs. You probably will never get a cat to fetch a newspaper, bring in the mail, or personally deliver your bedroom slippers. Feline brains don't seem to work that way. Beyond the reach of your arm, a cat is on its own. When the cat is out of your reach, even your most heartfelt commands will likely have zero impact.

In other words, you are welcome to stand ten feet from your cat and yell, "Sit!" But don't expect anything. To teach a cat and coax it to perform, you must be able to touch the animal.

THE TRAINING TABLE

That's why, for training sessions, I recommend putting the cat on a training table. Any sort of table, desk, or workbench will do.

Training on the floor is also possible, provided you don't mind kneeling or hunkering down. But even if your knees are younger than mine, you may be more fleet-footed from a standing position, rather than having to crawl on all fours every time your animal darts away. And particularly before obedience training, cats will dart.

None of this is meant to detract in any way from the innate intelligence of cats. They're smart. There is perhaps no better testimony to their wisdom than the fact that they have collectively hoodwinked the human race. For years, cats have duped us into believing that they cannot be trained to perform.

Unlike dogs, who are so ready to wag their tails exuberantly over their humans, cats have kept us in our places. We must work for their affection. They're choosy. They're aloof.

When you are training your cat, this will work to your advantage. Because trick-performing domesticated cats are so rare, anything your cat learns will be considered unusual. And you, as the teacher, will be considered a genius.

As one way of shattering the cats-can't-be-trained tradition, I line up six of my cats on the same table at the

The Cat Chorus Line

same time. They sit on their little fannies. They can't kick like the Rockettes. But I've yet to hear a catcall for calling this my own "Cat Chorus Line."

Today my cats are among the best-known performing felines in the country. However, I am far from the first individual to prove that domesticated cats can be trained. That honor may go to a gentleman I never met who was staging shows some thirty-five or forty years ago. He would dress his two cats in boxing trunks and paw-size gloves, then place them in a customized ring for a miniature prizefight.

I have read nothing of this gentleman's methods, but I would suspect that before he taught his cats to perform, he was able to hold them. As a prelude to training, cats must be held and touched.

With some pets, this takes time.

YOUR CAT SHOULD BE RELAXED

Early in my cat-training career, when I spent every available moment thinking up new ways to get potential buyers of cat houses into my store, I would run classified ads in the Mundelein newspaper. Bring me your cat, leave it, and I'll teach it something, I promised.

No cat ever flunked its training. I remember one particularly impossible specimen. Aloof, with a capital *A*, this feline might have been happier on his own planet. But on and off for days, I tried to hold him and pet him. Whenever I was within arm's reach, I would put my hands on the animal and speak to him in a soft voice. The cat's fright predated his stay at my shop. Therefore, I wanted to be especially reassuring.

After a few days, the animal became less frightened. After a few weeks, he calmed down to the point where he was a perfectly relaxed cat. In the process, he learned to sit, lie down, roll over, and play dead. I was actually sorry to see him go.

But sadly, the next time I saw him at a show, where he was being judged on looks and body structure and not on disposition, the animal had reverted to its skittish former self. With no one figuratively pulling out the ham, he had stopped doing tricks. After observing his owner and talking with her, I could understand why. She was fond of the animal and certainly not physically abusive, but she showed the cat no warmth or affection.

How people raise their pets is a matter of personal preference. Granted, there are some cats that are like some people—they have behavior problems, no matter how well intentioned their house mates. But most often, to have and keep a friendly pet, you only have to be friendly to the animal.

PRETRAINING CONTACT

You have to put your hands on your cat. You have to pick it up and hold it. When your animal is used to being loved in this way, it is also ready to be trained.

Some cats will never be ready. If your cat positively refuses to be held in your arms, no matter how often you try, spare yourself and the cat further agony. In all likelihood, the cat will not adapt well to a training program, which stresses frequent and concentrated contact between the human and the animal. Such contact might create an intolerable situation for the cat and, consequently, for you. These cats can be sweet and loving in their own way and on their own terms. But do not try to turn them into performers.

I am frequently asked which breeds are the most trainable. My own troupe members have been mixed breeds and Scottish Folds; it's just worked out that way. But overall, the worse the blood lines, the better the trainability. By temperament, a "Heinz 57-variety cat" may be best adjusted and easiest to train.

However, this is not always true. On numerous occasions, people have dared me to teach anything to a Siamese cat. One Indiana state patrolman was notably adamant. "George, you're just fine and dandy. Your cats are really great," he said. "But you couldn't teach my cat a thing."

The patrolman owned several Siamese kittens. He thrust one forward. I worked with it several minutes, which was long enough to teach it to sit down and lie down. The disbelieving patrolman, his mouth open wider than a hungry Saint Bernard's, shuffled away.

Another time, I was interviewing two little girls on my cable TV program. Both had won titles in beauty pageants. Their cats, which were littermates, were mostly Siamese. As I talked with the girls, I worked with one of their cats. I kept petting him and turning him over. Suddenly, I sat back in my chair, threw out my arms, and announced that the cat was ready to perform. Before a live studio audience, the previously untrained animal played dead. He lay on his back with all four paws in the air. The audience roared.

Persian cats, in contrast, are among the most difficult to train. They're too relaxed. They're like rag dolls. You pick them up and they droop. It's possible to train a Persian cat, but you probably would not be able to teach it ten or twelve tricks. Instead, depending upon your persistence and patience, you could teach it enough to prove to your friends that you're a remarkable cat trainer. But stick with the basic tricks such as sitting down, lying down, playing dead, rolling over, and begging. How much further you are able to go will depend upon your relationship to the animal.

HOW LONG SHOULD TRAINING SESSIONS LAST?

It doesn't work to push a cat too far. If you do, you stand a good chance of losing it as a potential performer. It will come to hate the training sessions.

Cats, however, have a built-in rescue device—namely, a short attention span. Plan to work with a cat no more than five to ten minutes at a time. Most likely, you won't need to consult a stopwatch. When a training session begins, most cats will be interested. They'll be curious. They'll wonder what you're going to do and what they'll have to do to please you.

Cats really do try to please their owners. As humans, we do things for other people. Cats are no different, although, if I had to put their attitude into words, it would probably be: Oh, well, let's pacify this individual who claims to own us; as we know, we really own him. Let's give him a break and do a little something for him.

But when cats tire, this spirit of cooperativeness

vanishes. After five to ten minutes of training, their interest will flag. They'll be distracted, tired, and bored. They'll have other things on their minds, like nap time. Whether you're finished or not, the training session has ended. If you try to work with a cat beyond this point, it won't perk up—and may not show up—for the next training session.

Ideally, using the step-by-step methods outlined in the following chapters, you will train your cat five to ten minutes an hour, every hour, as many times as you can squeeze into a day. I say "ideally"; I know that's not possible for everyone.

Naturally, the more time you spend training your cat, the more quickly you will see results. But if round-the-clock training sessions, every hour on the hour, are not practical for you, there is no reason not to train your cat at a more leisurely pace.

Those following the ideal schedule might complete six or seven sessions daily. The next day you repeat the same schedule. This is the procedure I follow when I'm preparing a new cat to join the act. So long as I'm going to be with the animal all day anyway, I don't find it difficult to set aside the time. That's why, I'm sure, I have such good luck training new cats during cat shows. For hours on end, there we are, at the same booth.

But again, cat training is meant to be enjoyable. To keep it that way, select a schedule that fits your life-style.

Moreover, remember your cat's needs. Cats love to snooze. Every time you turn around, they seem to be asleep. Cats doze away almost 65 percent of their time. Within a twenty-four-hour period, most cats sleep on and off for nearly fifteen hours; and that's when they don't have anything more strenuous to do than eat, play, and jump on the windowsill. Training sessions and performing may tire your cat. Don't make excessive demands on the animal. Otherwise, the cat will be half asleep. When my cats are performing at home or on the road, I never schedule more than two shows per day. Cats shows are generally on weekends. That means two shows on Saturday and two more on Sunday. From experience, I know the cats will not be at their best for the final show on Sunday. Oh, they'll do some tricks. But they'll do them slowly and they may eliminate more than they include. The cats will be tired. There's no getting around it. Being hauled in and out of the van and in and out of the exhibition hall, they have lost a lot of sleep. Showgoers tromping by have disturbed the cats' catnaps. They'll sleep all the way home in the van. The next day they'll sleep even more than usual. So will I.

"Hey," I always tell the audience at the start of the last show. "These cats are tired."

But since the animals still do much more than other domesticated cats, the crowd invariably thinks I'm fishing for compliments—and we get them. Invariably, our "late shows" are some of our most warmly received.

HOW OLD SHOULD MY CAT BE FOR TRAINING?

When you begin training your pet, work around the age of your cat. If you're like me, you acquire cats of no particular age through no particular plan of your own. At age two, Tasha proved to be one of the most difficult cats I would ever train. I was a greenhorn coach, and she has never had one of those get-up-and-go let's-conquer-the-world personalities. With Tasha, I spent arduous days on tricks that some of the younger cats later learned in a couple of sessions.

Using my methods, however, *Chicago Tribune* writer Mary Daniels taught Ashley, her six-year-old Russian blue, to jump through a hoop. Spurred on by the promise of chicken nuggets, the cat mastered the procedure in a matter of minutes.

In my experience, prime time to begin training is

when a kitten is eight weeks old. I've started with older cats, and I've started with younger ones. But eight weeks seems about perfect. At that stage, kittens are fairly strong and just at the point where they are used to people and about to enter cathood. Any sooner, they're still playful little kitties.

However, if your cat is two, three, four years, or older, there is no reason not to teach it to perform. Just be certain the cat is accustomed to being held.

PUTTING KITTENS IN THE MOOD FOR TRAINING

If you happen to have the animal from birth, there are several ways to prepare it for training. First, hold the kitten in your hands. Ever so gently, pet it with your fingers. A cat raised this way becomes a loving cat. That's how I raised Scupa. Even before his eyes were open, I began petting him.

Some mother cats positively will not allow humans to go near their kittens. Should you get too close, they will hiss, bite, scratch, get violent, and do whatever else it takes to keep you away. Abide by the mother cat's wishes. She is capable and protective. Do not upset her.

Some mother cats become so furious with humans that they pick up their kittens and hide them. The mother continues to care for her offspring. But in no uncertain terms, she has ordered, "Hands off!"

Misty, my daughter's cat, never did this. She would allow me, in her presence, to take Scupa and sit in a chair. Misty would be right there, watching, making sure I wasn't abusing her kitten. Scupa lived with his mother for eight weeks. Some people say that kittens can be taken from the litter at six weeks. I say that's too young.

Kittens can also be prepared for performing by getting a head start on obedience training. This means first learning to remain on the training table long enough to be taught something. First, hold the kitten in your hands. Then put it on a table. All the while, you're talking to it and petting it. "What a great cat you are," you keep saying. You want the kitten to believe it, and to act accordingly.

Next, take your hands away for a moment. As soon as the cat moves, your hands return, reassuringly. In this way, animals get used to remaining on the table. Initially, you make it worth their while. Feed them a treat while they're up there. You want the animal to feel comfortable on the training table.

STAY ON THE TABLE!

Whatever age your cat is, you will first have to teach the animal to stay on the table. You put the animal on the table. It scoots down. You retrieve it, pet it, and talk to it. It scoots down again. You retrieve it again. You offer food. Finally, the cat stays.

In front of an audience that expects a cat to do nothing, even staying on the table becomes something of a trick. In a more advanced variation, six cats play dead. The trick takes as long as it takes to turn the animals on their backs on the table. But the impact is long-lasting.

GETTING USED TO NOISE

As a preparation for training, noise toleration is vital, too. Cats-in-training must be able to concentrate as fully as possible on directions, and not be distracted by every outcry from the television set or ring of the telephone. Ideally, star felines are supposed to remain unrattled. My own cats live and train in my store and the adjoining workshop, where they've grown up with sawing, hammering, and stapling. Without that conditioning, I doubt that Victoria could have been wheeled in such tranquillity down Fifth Avenue in New York in a baby stroller.

If you live in a nice, quiet house in suburbia, I'm not suggesting that you bring in a brass band. But the normal sounds of daily living, occasionally heightened, can help noise-proof your animal. The next time your cat is in the kitchen, clang some pots. Bang a lid. Knock a tin plate off the counter. At first the animal is likely to be spooked by the clatter. Startled, it will fly out of the room. But repeat the process.

Especially at feeding time, when your animal acts ravenous—no matter how much it ate just a short time earlier—drop the unbreakable plate again. In time, the cat will be ruled by its stomach and stay put. If you're serious about bringing in a brass band, this is the time to do it.

There is no need to give yourself a splitting headache. But the more clamor your cat becomes accustomed to, especially from an early age, the better adjusted it will be. This is a definite plus for performers and nonperformers alike.

CAR TRAVEL

Further, you can help prepare your kitty for its own "Amateur Hour" by taking it for rides in the car. If you're going to be traveling to shows someday, the cat will have to get there. My own cats have never shown a dislike for travel. However, I have heard of some felines' being completely traumatized by cars. At least one family, about to relocate across town, went to the vet for a tranquilizer. Only when the family's cat was slightly benumbed could it be coaxed into the car and, subsequently, into the new home.

My method is pain-free. As preparation for interstate travel, I simply take the cats joy riding. The first time I took Scupa, he was six weeks old. He sat in my lap. I drove him to see my store. Then I returned him to his mother.

Now, after a steady diet of love, human contact,

"My cats have never shown a dislike for travel."

noise, and occasional sightseeing trips, you and your cat are ready to being the actual training.

WHO SHOULD DO THE TRAINING?

Logically, the best person to do the teaching is the one who has the best rapport with the animal. Usually, this is the individual who does the feeding. However, there can be additional factors.

In the world of felines, there are women's cats and men's cats. Regardless of the cat's gender, some animals seem to respond more readily to female humans than to males, or vice versa. You will have no trouble making the determination. In whose lap does the cat do the most snoozing? On whose chair is the cat most likely to be curled?

Should your cat display a clear-cut preference, honor it. As two-legged creatures about to attempt to impose our will on some of the most individualistic members of the four-legged set, we need every advantage we can get.

The "gender preference" of cats frequently dates back to their early days. Tasha is strictly my cat. There is no one she likes better. When Charlene is working at my store, Tasha will put up with her; that's the extent of it. Still, I credit Tasha with being inordinately practical. Should anything happen to me—her one and only—I have no doubt she would adjust. She would fall for someone else, presumably another male.

Now consider the case of a longtime bachelor and his longtime companion, a cat. They live together happily. Then the bachelor marries. His bride moves in with all her gear. No matter how solicitous the new wife may be, there is a good chance that the cat will view her as a meddler. He may despise her. Eventually, he may simply dislike her.

HOW CATS ADAPT TO NEWCOMERS AND CHANGES

It has been my experience that cats don't necessarily become jealous when new cats are brought into the family. Tasha adjusted, with minimal moping, to Miss Hiss. Tasha and Miss Hiss didn't seem to mind when I added Madame Tanya, and so on and so on. Oscar was different. When he saw Scupa the first time—when I drove Scupa to the store for a visit—Oscar hissed. Oscar—strong and usually silent, but this time demonstrative—reached over and swatted Scupa with his paw (Scupa was not hurt).

I never found out if they would have mended their fences. Not long after, Oscar disappeared.

My troupe members usually adapt to newcomers. As many times as I've acquired another cat, I just bring it into the store. Once someone did me one better. Like a foundling in a basket, a cat was left in a box at my back door. Later, a man called. His wife was allergic. Between red eyes and a runny nose, she couldn't live with the cat anymore. That's all the man said.

The cat was gorgeous—a Russian blue, or mostly Russian blue—and about two years old. What a monster. He weighed ten or twelve pounds. I taught him to sit and lie down, and was prepared to keep him and possibly work him into the act. But I was worried. This time Scupa was the disagreeable party. He wrestled with the new cat. I saw animosity. Fortunately I heard about a woman who had called the Orphans of the Storm animal shelter in Deerfield. She wanted a grayish cat. She got one.

More often, when I bring in a new cat, the senior troupe members will growl. That lasts a few days. I keep my eye on them. Until the new acquisition grows brave, it usually hides under the desk or in a cat house. The others don't attack. They do hiss. But finally the cats seem to realize that the new boarder is to be permanent. Most of the grousing stops.

My cats play together. Scupa and Valentine will roll around and chase each other. They growl, but without a chord of intimidation, and jump up on top of the cat furniture. Victoria and Spooker do the same thing. Such frolics last about fifteen minutes, after which the tuckered-out cats fall asleep.

Meanwhile, The Hisser just glares, surrounded by an impenetrable, if imaginary, wall. The other cats have nothing to do with her. They wouldn't dare play with her and they're too smart to attack her. The Hisser's domain, so far as she's concerned, is the whole store. In the trick I call "The Queen and Her Court," she is guarded by cat guards; they keep their distance.

All my cats eat from the same large bowl and water dish. Only when the others have finished do The Hisser and Tasha make their entrance. They eat last and slowly. That's their style.

If you have one or more cats in your home, there are other considerations. Some cats become upset when you so much as rearrange a room. For six months, the sofa sat in the same spot; now it's on the opposite wall. Your cat is resentful.

At least temporarily, a cat's mood level may also dip when the family grows. Take the case of the longtime bachelor who marries. In time, he and his wife have a baby, who has a nursery. Suddenly, a once-docile cat snarls, repeatedly. A cat that never had litter-box problems begins defecating on the carpet.

The best thing to do at a time like this is give the cat extra attention and affection. Prove that you're not being neglectful. To solve the defecation problem, you may have to confine the cat in a room with its litter box for a time. Pray for peace. In the meantime, do not begin cat training. Wait for life to settle down.

Assuming that it does, regard training as a one-man or one-woman project. Even if you got your cat after you acquired your family, and the cat responds well to more

The Queen and Her Court

than one family member, select just one trainer. Cats learn by repetition. Why confuse them?

Two people, both following my training methods, still bring their own interpretations and complications. Suppose one trainer is right-handed and the other is left-handed. Generally, when a right-handed person places a cat in a standing position, he will face the cat to the left. A lefty may face the cat to the right. No wonder the animal scoots off the training table.

However, once a trick is learned, there is no reason why another family member or friend cannot follow your cues and lead the cat through an already-mastered procedure. This may be particularly rewarding to children, who are eager to show off their talented feline to friends.

On weekends when my own trained cats are booked in more than one city, my associate, Ed Zerr, becomes the stand-in coach. He takes a couple of cats to one locale while I take the rest of the troupe to another. Beyond the usual feline mischief during shows, Ed assures me that he has encountered no particular problems.

Still, it's the trainer who knows the cats best. Substitute coaches can do a fine job, but usually cannot get quite the performance from the animals that the trainer can.

THE IMPORTANCE OF REPETITION

To train a cat, you more or less lay a procedure down in its brain. You repeat the same thing many, many, many, many times.

The tricks in the following chapters have been dissected step by step. Do not expect to sail through a whole trick in a day. This may happen sometimes, but that depends upon your cat, and upon you. With some tricks, the animal may require several sessions or days on a single step.

Then, at the start of each new training session, go back and review what the cat has already learned. Feline learning is cumulative. Like people, cats build on what they already know.

Before a cat learns to roll over—with your coaxing— on the training table, it must learn to lie down. And for you to depend on a cat to lie down for more than a split second, the animal must master staying on the table.

BUILD LOGICALLY ON PREVIOUS TRICKS

Some tricks build directly on previous tricks. Other stunts involve just one set of actions, which should be tailored to the cat's stage of development. Jumping through a hoop is a good example. Because the growth plates in a kitten's skeleton have not closed, the animal should start out by jumping from one spot to another, not more than six inches apart. You don't want to risk a fractured leg. Then as the animal gets older and its bones become more stable, both the distance and the height at which the cat jumps through the hoop can be increased. Some of my cats soar several feet.

Training more than one cat at the same time is something I have never done, although I suppose it's possible. A better policy, I'd say, is to train one cat as fully as possible, and then train the other. Later, on the cat-show circuit, you will find that having more than one trained performer is an asset. That way, you won't have to put all your eggs in one basket, or hopes on one feline. To avoid possible jealousy, step up the number of times you pick up and pet the animals that are not yet in training.

With any cat, there is no problem telling whether a trick is mastered. If the animal does the trick once, it's his. He may choose not to do it every time, but he still knows it.

ON DAYS AND OFF DAYS

Certainly, cats have good days and bad days. At a show in Albuquerque, I must have spent half my time chasing Valentine and Miss Hiss. They were all over the place. One thousand pairs of arms could not have restrained them. I had the whole audience in the act. They kept scooping up the cats and bringing them back up to the stage.

At other shows I may have one prima donna—which one, varies—that absolutely refuses to do her tricks. At such times, I am thankful to have more than a one-cat troupe. Unquestionably, when a feline decides not to do something, there is only one thing that you, as a mere mortal, can do. Turn to the audience and shrug, "Oh, well, cats will be cats. And who said they could be trained anyway?"

If I'm lucky, another troupe member will salvage my reputation. Most of the time, one does.

When you're training cats, it's important never to lose your temper. It won't do any good. You'll only scare the cat. And a frightened cat is gone, under the couch, under the bed, anywhere to avoid you. Save your reprimands.

Training an animal to do tricks is not like teaching it right from wrong.

Scupa, a little devil if there ever was one, is quickly learning about the latter. Lately, he has taken to running out the door of my shop. I can't put up with that; he could be lost or hurt. So I go running after him. I spank him, certainly not with any force, but enough to show him that he's being corrected. Then he gets mad at me and he pouts. He ignores me.

With many cats, problem behavior includes nibbling on electrical cords and jumping on countertops and tables other than their training tables. Such behavior may call for discipline.

IF DISCIPLINE IS NEEDED

There are several approaches to disciplining your pet. To keep an animal away from cords and other wires, try the special sprays and creams you can get from pet stores. The taste of these products is supposed to repel the cats. If sprays and creams don't work, try rubbing a bar of soap over the cords. Cats generally despise soap.

If countertops and tables become a problem, roll up several sheets of newspaper. Every time you spot your cat where you'd prefer him not to be, slap down the newspaper alongside him—not on him. You are reacting to an unacceptable behavior. You never want to hurt the animal.

Another tool is the water gun. Cats relish a bowl of water, but find nothing enjoyable about a sudden squirt. If your cat jumps up where he shouldn't, startle him with a spurt of water. He'll get the idea. As a last disciplinary resort, raise your voice. This is a strong register of disapproval, especially to a cat raised on praise.

THE IMPORTANCE OF PRAISE

When we praise cats, we're on a lot firmer ground. Praise is an essential component of teaching tricks. You talk in a calm, soothing voice and laud the animal so often that it becomes automatic: You're smart. You're gorgeous. You're wonderful!

Perhaps your cat has mastered ten tricks. Onstage one day, it may do just six or seven. Still, you have to feel gratified. Later, go back to the skipped tricks. The cat may or may not have changed its mind.

And should there be a trick that your cat consistently refuses to attempt or execute, bypass the trick altogether. Be realistic. You are the trainer, but you still take your cues from your cat. Enough tricks have been included in this book that there is no need for you and/or the cat to become upset about any one maneuver.

Given your pet's reputation for independence, you may find this next statement hard to believe. But cats are sensitive to failure. That's one of the main reasons I have pretty much retired Tasha from the performance circuit. By the time a cat is five or six years old, it has lost much of its effectiveness onstage. An older cat slows down, and Tasha was slow to start with. Now if I ask her to do something and she refuses, I'm embarrassing her. I don't feel right putting her in those situations.

Far healthier, for both you and the animal, is to build feline pride. Cats feel good when they do something right. For some of the more advanced tricks, like eating from a high chair and playing the piano, the cats are motivated by food, which becomes their reward.

For all the tricks, they are praised and petted. When you pet, pet gently. The animal will feel good and know that you care. Pet the cat all along its back. Consider the tail a reminder. When you get that far, go back to the cat's head and start over again.

We love our cats. If we didn't, there would be no reason to spend time training them.

In the following chapters, we shall take up individual trick in detail, starting with the simpler ones and then moving on to more elaborate feats.

4. Building a Repertoire: The First Tricks to Teach

Your cat's first trick will be to learn to sit down. This is the equivalent of kindergarten: without mastery of sitting, there can be no promotions.

Sit Down

Your cat is at least eight weeks old. You have picked it up often and petted it frequently. The cat does not shy away from your touch. Training will require frequent and concentrated contact between the trainer and the animal.

While it may be tempting to make cat training a family

project, use just one trainer. Later, once a trick is mastered, as we have seen, others can coax the cat through the maneuver.

Your cat has grown accustomed to noise. This will come in handy when you perform before groups. But for training, you—the trainer—may be more at ease in a quiet area, free from the very distractions your cat now tolerates. For this reason, a bedroom, basement, or other less trafficked area of your house or apartment will be ideal.

Remember that cats have short attention spans. Depending upon your cat's interest and energy, each training session will last from five to ten minutes. If this is too much for your pet, start with a shorter session. Ideally, you will train every hour on the hour, six or seven times a day, and repeat the schedule the following day for as long as it takes to learn a trick. If this is impossible, train as often as you can.

When your cat has finished a training session, you'll know it. Most likely, the cat will lose interest or scamper off the table.

Any table, desk, or workbench is fine for your training table. However, do not select something that is otherwise off-limits for the cat. If you've been trying for months to keep your pet off the dining-room table, don't use it for training. It's pointless to undo your previous disciplining. Moreover, you will want the cat to build positive associations with the table. When the cat is on the table, trick time has begun. Some people may prefer to train on the floor, but, as I've mentioned before, I find this a more difficult position from which to retrieve a surefooted cat.

Obedience training will cut down your number of retrievals. Cats must learn to stay—whether sitting, standing, or lying—on the table before they can learn tricks. If the cat is always running away, how can you teach him anything?

Obedience training can begin long before trick training. Simply put your kitten or cat on the training table.

Keep your hands on the animal as you talk to him, pet him, and praise him. Take your hands away for a moment. When the animal moves, put your hands back on him. Continue petting, praising, and talking. Periodically remove your hands. If the animal jumps down, retrieve him. Further entice your pet to stay on the table with his favorite snack, to be given as a reward while he is on the table. Repeat this conditioning as often as possible.

For some cats, staying on the training table is second nature. For others, it may take getting used to. There is no specific time limit that indicates whether your cat will stay in place on his own. But when you are confident that the animal will remain on the table, while you are at arm's length but with your hands off the cat, then you are both ready for trick number one: Sit Down.

By that time, the cat will be so used to the training table that a reward of food will no longer be necessary.

To teach the cat to sit:

1. Place the cat on the training table. No reward should now be necessary. During all training sessions and performances, remain no farther than arm's length from your pet. Don't be too trusting.

2. Stand the cat up on all four paws (Tasha, my semiretiree, is so used to sitting that sometimes the trick is getting her to stand). Be aware of the direction in which you are facing the cat. It makes no difference if the animal's head is next to your right hand or left. Just be consistent. Face the animal in the same direction every time you stand him up.

3. Place one hand under the cat's chin and the other on top of the cat's fanny. Gently push the animal into a sitting position.

4. All the while, say, "Sit. Sit. Sit."

5. All the while, praise the animal.

Keep practicing. Repetition is vital. Using this method, there are some cats I can teach to sit in a few minutes.

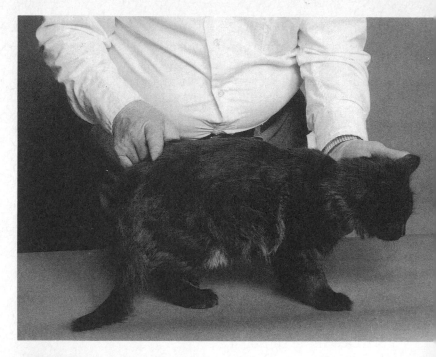

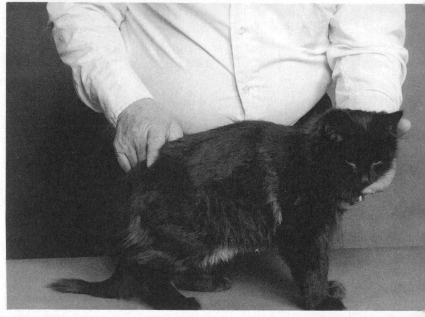

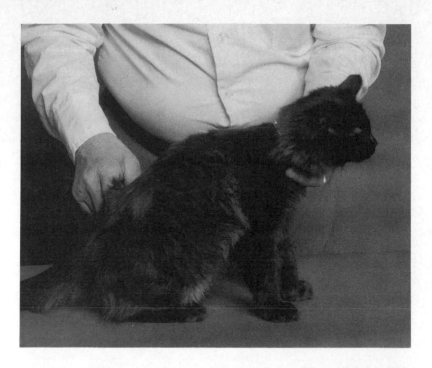

Teaching Sit Down. (*Above, left*) Stand the cat on the training table, always facing in the same direction. (*Left*) Put one hand lightly under the cat's chin and the other on its fanny. (*Above*) Gently push it into a sitting position. Say, "Sit. Sit. Sit." Praise the cat. Keep practicing until the cat's attention span ends.

Others require days of five- to ten-minute sessions, as many as possible in each twenty-four-hour period.

With this trick, you want to get your animal to the point that you can say, "Sit down," and it does. If this doesn't happen, there is nothing wrong with emphasizing your command with a light tap on the cat's fanny and/or chin.

The first time the cat sits down—with minimal or no assistance from you—the cat "owns" the trick. The animal may not sit for you every time, but you know he can do it. Proceed to the next trick.

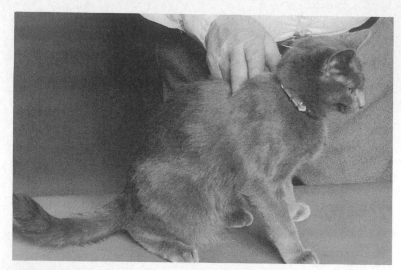

Teaching Lie Down. Place your hand, or your index and middle fingers, on the cat's shoulder blades.

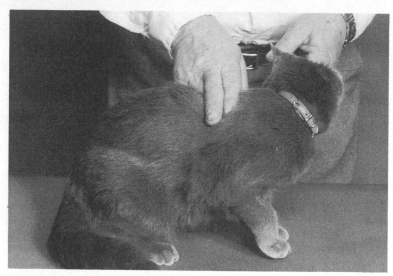

Gently push the cat down . . .

Lie Down

This trick is a direct outgrowth of the previous one. Although lying down and snoozing are a cat's two most

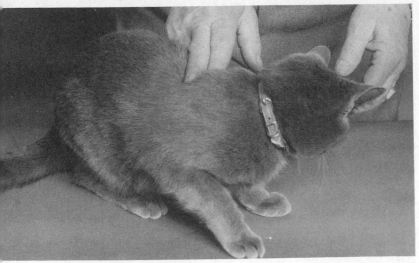

. . . and keep saying, "Lie down,"

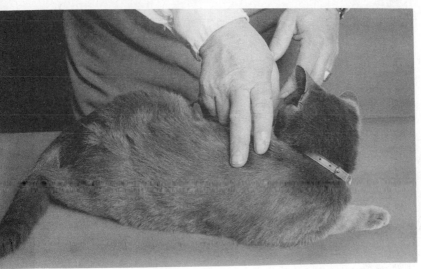

. . . until it is lying on the table. Praise the cat and stroke its back.

time-consuming pastimes, Lie Down as a stunt is memorable. Remember, most people have never seen a domesticated cat do a single trick.

As in all the tricks, place your cat on the training table.

1. Place your hand, or just your index and middle fingers, on the cat's shoulder blades.

2. Gently push the cat down until it is lying down.

3. All the while, keep saying, "Lie down."

4. As always, praise the animal profusely. Stroke its back.

Unlike sitting, this is not a trick that cats ordinarily do on command. Even upon mastery—doing the trick once with minimal assistance—animals probably will continue to require a tap or gentle push on the shoulder blades. Persistence on your part will also be required.

Don't settle for a crouch. Keep practicing until your animal goes flat. In the beginning, many cats do a modified Sit Down with a slightly lowered back. This is not enough. Always pushing gently, petting and praising the animal, encourage the cat to keep stretching its front legs farther and farther out front. Your goal, if not the cat's, is to have those front legs flat on the table. As in Sit Down, the back legs will remain tucked underneath. Although the position may be sleep-inducing, most cats keep their heads up during the trick. They will not doze on the spot.

One of the most winsome aspects of this trick is the way it has been personalized by every cat I've trained. Tasha, perfectly in character, takes her good old time, slowly stretching out her front legs. Valentine, ever frisky, never lies down. She plops.

Roll Over

Other than the early steps of obedience training, this is the first trick that uses food as a reward. Cats do not customarily roll from side to side on command. That's why we use the treat—it's a not-so-subtle inspiration.

For Sit Down and Lie Down, praise is an adequate reward. But in Roll Over, you're asking the cat literally to extend itself and do something much more unusual. And when you're doing the asking before an audience, it helps to have something to elicit the desired behavior speedily enough that you don't lose the crowd's attention. Besides, I've never met a cat that turned down a treat.

To teach your cat to roll over:

1. Stand the animal on the training table. The cat's side is facing you.
2. Reach around the animal to the two legs farthest from you. Hold the legs and turn the cat on its side.
3. Still holding the animal with one hand, use your other hand to hold a favorite treat in front of its nose. Don't reward the animal yet.
4. When you're sure your cat isn't squirming off anywhere—food is a fine attention-grabber—let go of the animal. But using one hand, move the food across the cat's shoulder. Be just quick enough to keep the food back far enough that the animal must roll to its side to be rewarded.
5. Now, going in the other direction, pull a treat across the cat's nose. Once again, it should roll.

Aim for the day when you can coax the cat to roll in both directions, all for the same treat.

There are many theories about treats and the general feeding of performing animals. Some trainers tell me they do not feed their animals for twenty-four hours before a performance on the assumption that a hungry performer is also a performer with lots of incentive.

Phooey! To me, that's cruel and unusual punishment. I could never treat my cats that way. There are only two appetite-related concessions I make. First, when I'm going to be teaching a trick like Roll Over, which is dependent

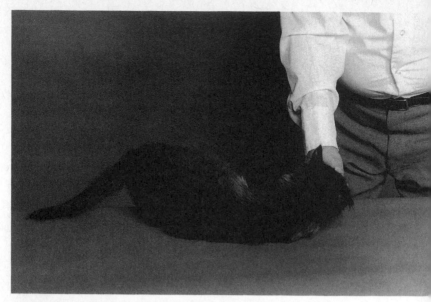

Teaching Roll Over. From a standing position, turn the cat on its side.

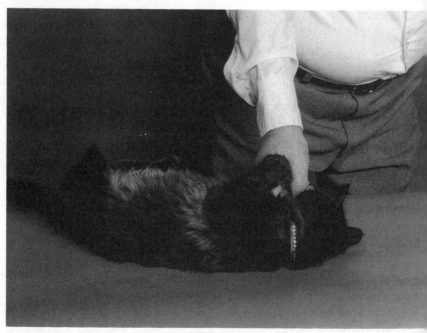

Hold a favorite treat in front of the cat's nose.

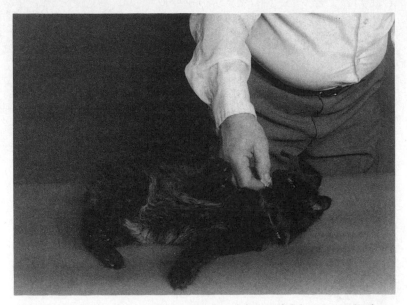

Move the treat across the cat's shoulder quickly enough that the animal must roll to the other side to be rewarded.

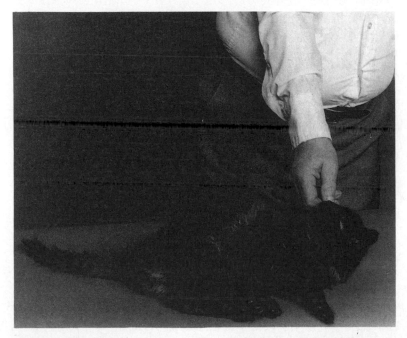

Reverse this move for the cat to roll back in the opposite direction.

on a reward of food, I schedule the first training session early in the morning, before the cat has eaten. After the training session, I feed the animal as usual.

Second, if my troupe is scheduled to perform, I feed the cats, but slightly less than normal. One look at my animals and you know they're far from starved. But if the cats are going to be doing two shows a day, two days in a row, and they are going to be somewhat tired after their ride to the show in my van, I find that with a tinge of hunger, they are apt to perform better. On the other hand, if they're sluggish from a full stomach and tired, too, it's hard to get them to do much.

At home, on the days we practice tricks utilizing rewards, I feed the cats their full ration of canned cat food, but put out a little less dry food, which they use as a between-meal nibble.

Unlike dogs, cats generally do not clean out a food dish all in one sitting or standing. More mannerly, they'll have a bit at a time, then return later. But treats are different. Even when my cats don't feel like performing, they always make room for a snack.

Play Dead

If your cat adores rolling over on its back to have its tummy rubbed, much of your training for this trick is already completed. I also call this trick "Cat-a-Back."

1. Stand the cat on the training table, with its right side or left side facing you. Be consistent. Always stand the animal in the same direction.
2. Reach around the animal, placing your hands around the bottom of the cat's two legs farthest from you. Holding these legs, lift slightly to turn the animal on its side.

3. Still holding those legs, continue turning until the animal is on its back.

4. As always, keep talking, praising, and reassuring your pet.

5. Depending on how fidgety your cat is, remove one hand and use it to rub the cat's tummy. For some felines, this is pure heaven. Continue to rub, talk softly, and praise. You're trying to relax your cat.

Should the cat squirm to its side, have your hands ready to return the animal to its back. The key will be whether the cat likes the "Cat-a-Back" position. This isn't something a cat merely tolerates. The animal either likes it or doesn't. Should the experience be traumatic for your pet, try another trick. However, with practice, most cats can learn this maneuver.

Don't keep your animal in the dark. Tell the cat exactly what you're doing and wishing: "My, you're a good cat! You're a quiet cat! You're a still cat! Now, you're going to play dead!"

When your cat is calm, step back a moment. As I describe this, I can almost hear the oohs and ahs from the audience. But remember, always keep the animal within arm's reach. Cats have nine lives. They're not going to play dead for long.

When you get the trick this far, it's quite effective. But if you can combine the stunt with noise toleration, it's dynamite. Once your cat is able to stay on its back, practice slapping your hand around the animal. With Scupa, I originally used this as a signal to stand up when the trick was over. But raised as he has been with the din of my shop and workshop, it didn't take long for the slapping sound to leave him unfazed. So I made that part of his trick.

Just picture normally playful Scupa, flat on his back, all four paws in the air. I'm slamming down my fist. And he doesn't move. Probably as a testimony to racket-filled

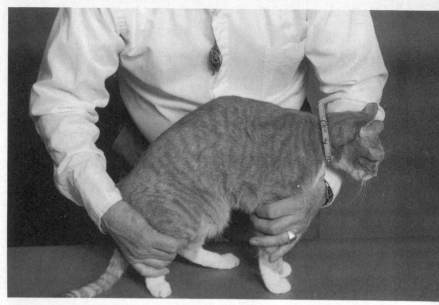

Teaching Play Dead. With the cat standing on the table, reach around and hold the cat's two legs farthest from you.

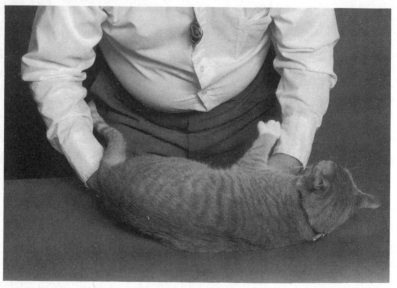

Lift slightly to turn the animal on its side.

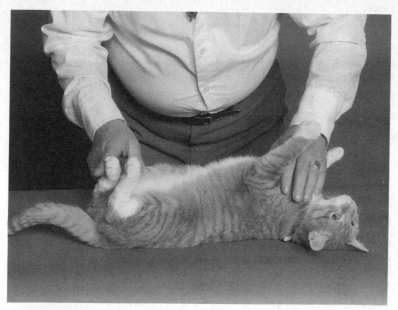

Keep turning until the cat is on its back.

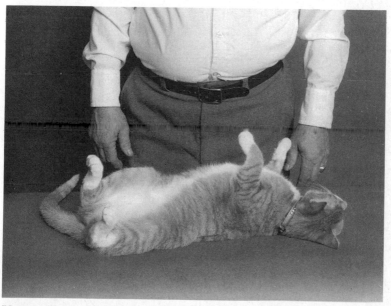

Keep talking, praising, and reassuring your pet.

upbringings, my other cats can do this, too.

I can put six of them on the same table, all on their backs. I slam down my hands and not a one moves—or not a one usually moves. This sight is a favorite for newspaper photographers.

The Death-Defying Trick

This stunt is so named because fearless felines perform it without so much as a safety net.

As a prerequisite, your cat must be able to lie on its back and play dead.

Obtain a two-by-four about three feet long. Glue, tack, or staple a piece of carpet around the wood. This will give the cat a familiar texture, and hopefully some security.

"No net!"

(*Photo courtesy of Pioneer Press, Inc., Mundelein, Illinois*)

1. Balance the carpeted two-by-four on two objects that rise several feet from the floor. Two flat-backed chairs, two benches, or two tables of equal height will be fine. Make sure the board is steady.

2. On the training table, turn the cat on its back and coax the animal to play dead.

3. In the playing-dead position, place the cat—still on its back—on the board. Keep your hands on the cat. Rub its tummy. Talk softly. Offer praise. The board is wide enough to accommodate the animal. The trick, of course, is getting the cat used to the board.

4. When your pet seems relaxed, remove your hands. Extol the animal's bravery.

Beg

It's perfectly natural for cats to come up on their hind legs. Innately inquisitive, they do it all the time for a closer look at any object higher than eye level. Now we will take that natural movement and put it in a different context.

In animals other than cats, going up on the hind legs is frequently associated with begging for food. So let's take the cat's treats, which are normally fed from a dish on the floor or right out of our hands, and lift up the treats. Presto, the cat is begging.

1. Put or command the cat into a sitting position.

2. With your hand, just run the treat—and make sure it's something the cat likes—in front of the animal's nose. Even a couldn't-possibly-be-hungry-again animal will catch the scent.

3. Now lift your hand and the cat will follow, right up on his hind legs. He wants that treat. Give it to him.

69

Teaching Beg. With the cat in a sitting position, run a treat in front of his nose.

Lift your hand and the cat will follow . . .

... **right up onto his hind legs. Reward him with the treat.**

The entire movement is swift. In fact, the hardest part may be holding on to the treat while your scent-spurred feline zips from a sitting position to standing on his hind legs, his body fully extended.

This is an easy trick, but a guaranteed crowd-pleaser. Most cats love it, too. They'll cradle your hand in their paws and lick and nibble your fingers.

Obviously, this trick is best executed when a cat is hungry. But for the promise of a treat, most felines will beg anytime.

Shake Hands

Dog lovers always get a kick out of it when Rover extends his paw. Getting a cat to do the same thing is a real accomplishment. This is an advanced trick.

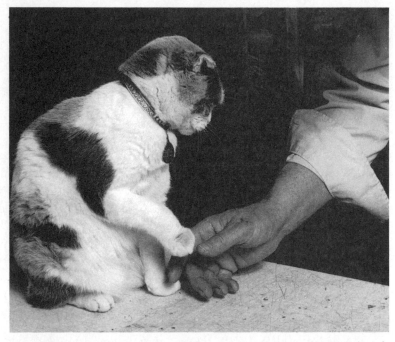

Learning to Shake Hands. With one finger, tap the inside of the sitting cat's front leg just above the paw.

1. Place the cat on its fanny or ask the animal to sit down.

2. Face the cat. Using one finger, reach over and tap the inside of one of the cat's front legs, just above the paw.

3. When mildly inconvenienced, many cats will simply raise the paw, and move backward. Or, never losing a step, they will lift the paw and continue walking forward. What you want is for the animal to extend its paw long enough so that you can stretch out your hand and shake. This is tricky. It may not happen. Shaking hands with your cat is a matter of patience, much of it your own. Nonetheless, continue to praise your animal. Talk to it. Pet it. Every time you reach across for the paw, you can easily rub the cat's chest.

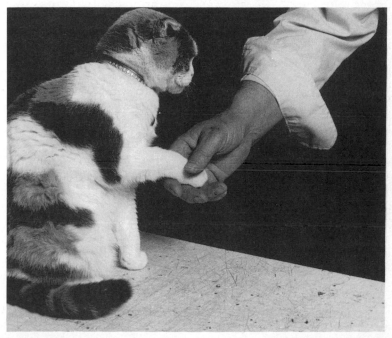

You want your pet to keep sitting and extend its paw for you to shake.

Despite the difficulty of this trick, training fosters closeness between you and your animal. The cat has your undivided attention. Don't be surprised if, even off the training table, the cat wants to spend more time with you.

Should progress on this trick be slow, don't get frustrated. Harsh words will hinder, not help, the learning process. If you or your cat become aggravated, skip this trick.

Tasha is the only one of my cats that extends her paw all the time. During her performing days, Madame Tanya would periodically comply. Oscar never shook my hand. Valentine and Miss Hiss won't either.

One caution: The easiest way to do this trick would seem to be reaching across and taking your cat's paw. For easygoing, I-love-anybody dogs, this might work. But it won't with cats. After endless repetitions with Tasha, she taught me the sequence: the human taps, the cat offers its paw, and you both shake.

After all that, give yourself a round of applause.

When your cat has mastered the seven tricks I've outlined in this chapter, it can fairly qualify as an unusually well-trained feline. Your friends are bound to be impressed, especially considering that most people believe that cats cannot be trained at all. These tricks are also very effective to present in the opening portion of a more extensive, public trained-cat act. But your cat's education has just begun. With further training, it can go on to increase its repertoire with many still more elaborate and impressive feats. I'll take up the art of teaching your feline these more advanced stunts in the next chapter.

5. "Presenting in the Center Ring..."

Many of the tricks in this chapter involve entertaining situations and the use of colorful props to enhance the humanlike appeal of your cat's actions. Let's lead off with a stunt that circus lions and tigers do all the time. Why shouldn't their domesticated kinfolk do it as well?

Jump Through a Hoop

This trick is both impressive and fairly simple to teach. If you have time to teach your cat no other trick using a showy prop, this one is a must.

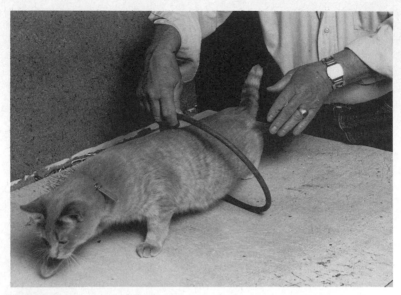

Jump Through a Hoop. With a treat on one end of the training table and the cat on the other, start by luring him to walk through the hoop.

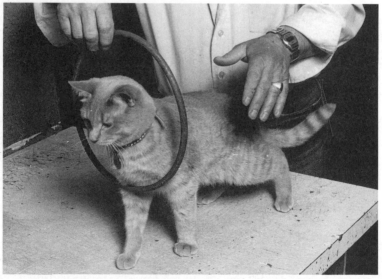

After he's walked through a few times, raise the hoop to get him used to jumping through to reach the treat.

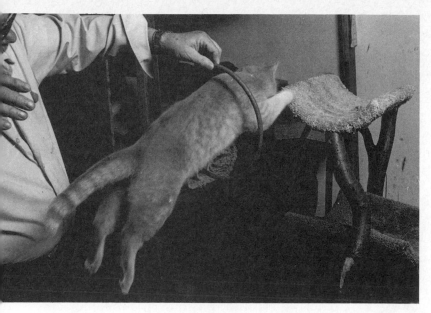

With the treat farther away and on a higher level, the cat learns to soar through the hoop.

Again, a reward of food will be necessary. The only required piece of equipment is a hoop. A medium-size embroidery hoop is fine. It's a good idea to decorate the hoop with colored ribbon to give a gay, circuslike effect. Otherwise, bend a wire coat hanger into a circle. I don't advise using large hoops: while the trick would be executed the same way, a large hoop detracts; it looks as if the cat is jumping through air, rather than hurling his body through a targeted area. He is hurling, but he's also salivating for the treat on the other side.

1. Put the cat on one end of the training table, some of his favorite food on the other, and the hoop in the middle.

2. Ask the cat, "Would you go through this hoop, please?" You want him to walk through. If he doesn't get the idea, pick up the treat, whisk it past his nose and put it back on the table. Coax the animal. If he still doesn't

seem to know which way to go, try to restrict the animal's path by stacking books around the table's perimeter. Once the cat walks through the first time, you've got it made. So does he. Give him a treat. Have him walk through several more times. Reward him.

3. Keeping the same setup, raise the hoop a couple of inches. This time you want the animal to jump through, or at least to raise his feet a little. If your student is a kitten, you won't want it to jump too high. Its skeletal growth plates have not closed yet. There will be plenty of time later for higher jumps.

4. If you're working with a grown cat, it's now time for "United Cat Lines" and "TW Cat." You want to increase the distance between the cat and the treat. In my shows, I place the treat on a cat perch on the training table. At home, you could position the treat on the training table and put the cat on a chair about three feet away. The chair, naturally, is lower than the table, so your rising star will have to soar.

Place the hoop midway between the cat and the table. "United Cat Lines. Zingo!"

Jump over the Baton

Get yourself a baton like those used by drum majorettes or band conductors. A magic wand, available from shops selling conjuring tricks, will also do.

1. This trick is similar to Jump Through the Hoop— only this time it's the cat on one end of the training table, the food on the other, and the baton in the middle. Hold the baton at the cat's chin level. The animal may jump over. I say "may" because, initially, cats never do. Their inclination is to go underneath.

2. Be quicker than the cat. As your pet tries to scoot

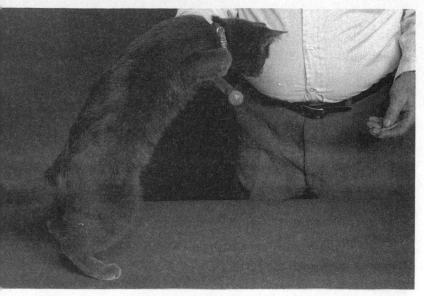

Jump over the Baton. By pressing a baton against your cat's chest, you can get him to jump over it to reach a tempting treat.

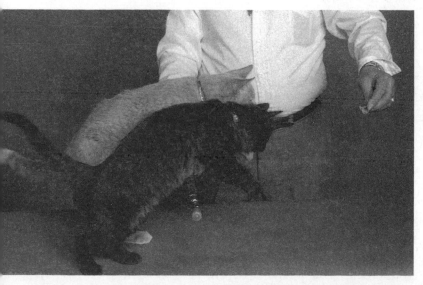

The Jump over the Baton trick takes time and repetition in training, especially with two felines in tandem.

under and get the food, gently press the baton against the animal. In this way, you are using the baton as a restraining device.

3. With the hoop trick, the first step was to get the cat to walk through it. Now, in exchange for stepping over the baton, you offer your pet the treat on the other side of the table.

4. Ultimately, you want the cat to jump over the baton. As in the other tricks, this takes practice and repetition.

One kitten, Spooker, was jumping over the baton when he was less than two months old. With him, the breakthrough came when he wanted the treat so much that the use of the baton as a restraining device became a source of bother for him. Deducing, I suppose, that there were only so many ways to get to the food, he finally jumped.

Cat Chorus

Even more appealing than one cat sitting on the table are two cats, or three, or more. The sight is so appealing, in fact, that no sequined leotards or top hats will be necessary (see illustration, p. 35). As feline choreographer and retriever (yes, part of the trick is keeping your chorus members in the chorus, and on the table), you will attempt to keep all feline fannies in some semblance of a straight line.

And one more thing. Troupers in this number must get along. No pawing or clawing of other chorines is permitted, and no cats need apply unless they can remain seated.

1. Sit one cat on its haunches. The cat can likely do this on command, but don't take the extra time. You are working against a two-handed stopwatch—brief feline attention spans and natural feline curiosity.

2. Seat the second cat next to the first. Repeat the process until all the cats are in line. How you position the cats—from right to left, left to right, center to the sides, or any variation—is not critical. Speed is. So is patience.

Plenty of times, I have three cats lined up on the table. I'm reaching for the fourth when two of the others jump off. Cat number four goes up, and another goes down. Work quickly and keep trying. The end result is a prime-time special.

Out to Dinner

Any cat can eat from a bowl on the floor. With this trick, your classy cat will be ready for a five-star restaurant—even if the restaurant is not ready for a four-legged patron.

Begin this trick any time after your cat has learned to sit down.

The required equipment is one chair with a back and an eating tray. A toy high chair or a baby's high chair (particularly if your baby has outgrown it) will be fine. I took a do-it-yourself approach, cutting down a cardboard tube, which I then assembled into a small chair and carpeted. If you're using a high chair, you will already have an eating tray. I made a small one out of wood, which fits on the arms of the chair.

1. Place the cat and the chair on the training table.

2. Put a bit of treat on the chair. This should entice the cat to jump in. If not, put the food in front of the cat's

Out to Dinner. With your cat and a do-it-yourself chair, or small high chair, on the training table, use a bit of food . . .

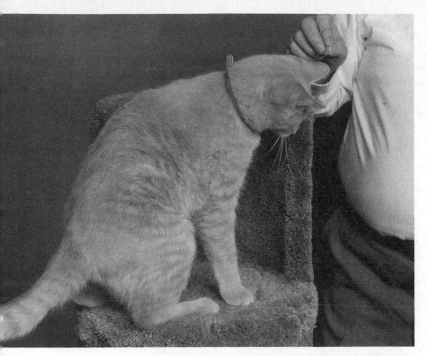

. . . to entice your cat to occupy the chair.

Once your pet is sitting up in the chair, with your reassurance and perhaps some chest-rubbing, . . .

. . . introduce a tray and a dish of food for a realistic dining-out act.

nose and then return the food to the chair. Your pet should get the idea.

3. Once the cat is in the chair, sit the animal up. No slouches on the training table! Reassure your pet. Praise him. Rub his chest.

4. Slide on the eating tray. The cat's front paws will be on the tray.

5. Immediately place some treat on the tray. With commendable manners, your cat will proceed to dine.

Operator, Please!

AT&T needs all the help it can get. How about a cat? Props this time are one lightweight plastic telephone, available at many drugstores and toy stores. Make sure that the treat you select as a reward is spreadable; cat food from the can will work nicely.

1. In full view and whiffing distance of your cat, remove the receiver from the phone and spread a little food on it, or on the portion of the phone that will be covered by the receiver.

2. Return the receiver to the telephone. You want the cat to make a concerted effort to knock the receiver off and thereby get the treat. In the beginning, help your pet. Forget about long distance. Place the phone next to the cat. Tilt the receiver up, so the animal gets the scent. Put the receiver down. The phone is lightweight. Even a kitten will be strong enough to knock down the receiver.

This is a cute trick. To draw the cat into conversation— or at least into the patter you carry on with the audience— take your thumb and lightly push some food into the telephone's mouthpiece or earpiece. This way, the cat should not only knock the receiver off but also lick it clean.

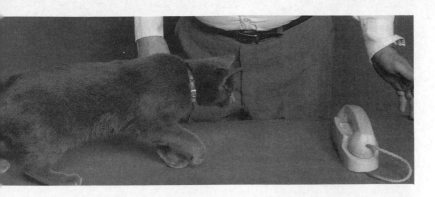

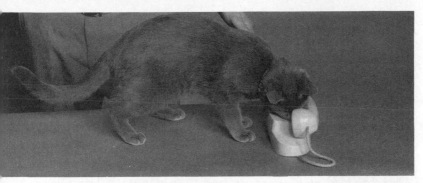

OPERATOR, PLEASE!

(*Top*) Spread a little food on or under the receiver of a lightweight, plastic toy telephone to attract the cat's attention. (*Center*) Help your cat, at first, to get the idea of removing the receiver from the phone to get at the treat. (*Above*) Put a little food in the telephone mouthpiece to complete the performance.

The Queen and Her Court

This stunt (see illustration, p. 48) utilizes three previous maneuvers—Sit Down, Out to Dinner, and Cat Chorus.

The trick is most effective with a small chair with a back. You could use a doll's high chair, but a queen should really not be that far from her subjects.

If one of your cats is a bit snootier than the rest, you will have the perfect throne sitter.

1. Place the "queen" in the chair. Sit her up. With any luck, she will demurely place her front paws on her lap.
2. Line up the other cats on either side of the throne. A Cat Queen is entitled to Cat Guards. Work quickly.

Queen Hiss, the supercilious Miss Hiss, has made headlines with this routine. From the start, she got right into the role, sometimes even flicking her tail in the faces of the Cat Guards. Most often, they put up with it. Onstage and elsewhere, nobody tangles with The Hisser.

Strolling Those Babies

This is always a hit. The trick incorporates both sitting and motion. It definitely falls into the category of advanced training. The required equipment is one baby stroller.

1. Seat your cat, on its fanny, in the stroller. This part should definitely be taught inside. Bend down and use your hand, as often as necessary, to restrain the animal. Praise the cat.
2. Gently move the stroller back and forth. This is the new component the trick introduces. Proceed slowly.
3. Stroll indoors with the animal.
4. Stroll outdoors, but with a restraining seat belt.

A Sociable Stroll

Usually, I put three of my cats in a stroller at a time. We've been down State Street in Chicago as well as Fifth Avenue in New York. In San Francisco, we strolled in the park at the cable car turnaround and on Fisherman's Wharf.

At cat shows, children in the audience stand in line. They all want to wheel the cats around.

Tchaikovsky Tomcat

You're welcome to use a real baby grand, but I'd recommend a child's toy piano. Tasha, pounding on hers, was pictured in *Cat Fancy* magazine.

The trick, as you'll discover, is not so much getting the cat to place his paws on the keyboard. Rather, the challenge is getting your pet pianist accustomed to the noise.

1. Bring the cat over to the piano. Earlier work with pots, pans, and tins should help.

2. As the trainer, start by playing a few notes. If the cat stays while you clang, the animal gets a treat.

3. Place the cat's paws on the piano. The setting is offbeat, but the position itself is not an unnatural one for felines. With the cat's paws on the piano, you continue playing. You want the cat to stay. If he does, reward him.

4. Next it's the cat's turn. His paws stay on the piano; yours are on the treat. This time, the cat must play for his supper. Move your hand, with the treat, across the cat's nose. Eventually, you want the animal to lift and lower his paws, thereby sounding the keys, as he reaches with his mouth for the food.

Tasha's technique has so developed that she does a not entirely unmusical crossover. On the keyboard, she will cross one paw over the other and continue to play. She aims not for Carnegie Hall, but for the treat in my fingers.

"Will you get in tune?"

Roll out the Barrel

This two-part trick is definitely advanced cat training. You will need one lightweight barrel, keg, or cylinder. I use a strong cardboard tube about twelve inches in diameter.

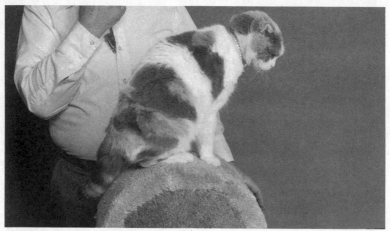

Roll Out the Barrel. In the first part of this two-part trick, the cat sits on top of the "barrel," a cardboard cylinder covered with carpeting.

As the barrel is rolled slowly backward, the cat moves forward to keep its equilibrium atop the barrel.

Other possibilities would be a round, lightweight waste-basket; the cylindrical container from a set of children's building blocks; or an empty two- or three-gallon card-board container. This can often be found at ice cream stores; just ask an employee to save you one.

In the second part of the stunt, the cat returns to the ground to "roll out the barrel."

Cover your container with carpet. Glue, tack, or staple the carpet in place. This will give the cat a soft surface, plus something to hold on to.

1. Turn the barrel on its side and place the cat on top. The cat should be facing you. Hold the cat with both hands. Pet the animal. Talk to it.

2. When your cat progresses to the point that it will remain on the barrel, at least momentarily, you can move one of your hands about an inch or two from the animal. With the other hand, slowly roll the barrel backward. You needn't roll far. Provided that the cat stays on the barrel, it will go backward as the barrel does. Retrieve the cat, as necessary, when it scampers down to the training table or floor. What you would like—and this may not be what you get immediately—is for the cat to walk forward as the Barrel moves backward. In this way, the animal will remain in its starting position on top of the barrel.

3. Help the animal walk forward by placing one hand under its fanny. Gently urge the cat forward as the barrel rolls backward.

4. Practice. Before progressing to the second part of the trick, which begins with step 5, the cat must be accustomed to the barrel.

5. Position your cat with its hind legs on the training table and its front paws on the barrel. Some cats may be more comfortable with their front paws and tummy on the barrel. The barrel remains sideways.

6. Place one hand on the barrel and the other near the cat's back. You want the cat to walk forward and, as it does, push the barrel. To help, slowly roll the barrel toward you. If the cat gets used to the idea of keeping its paws on the barrel, it will have to move its back legs forward. Pet and praise your cat.

Don't attempt to rush through the steps. This trick has been carefully dissected. Unfortunately, Tasha never showed me a shortcut to the end. However, it is possible to stop in the middle. If, after repeated training sessions, your cat refuses to adapt to steps 5 and 6, simply do the first part of the trick—and rename the sequence Roll on the Barrel.

Walking on a Leash

This is certainly worth a try, but cannot be taught to every cat. However, if your cat adapts, the reception is truly impressive. No one, but no one, expects to see a cat on a leash.

As a safety precaution, all cats should wear collars with identification tags. One way to teach this trick is to attach a leash to that collar. But a better way is to invest in a small harness that goes around the cat's neck and across its back. The harness, which is available at most pet shops, will in no way hurt the animal. I prefer it for this trick because the cat can't wriggle out. A leash may be attached right to the harness.

With a collar, in contrast, there is the possibility that if a cat really wanted to, it could slip free. Normally with a collar, the cat might put up a fuss for the first few minutes, then wear it without problems the rest of its life. But when you add a leash, the cat may protest. I prefer not to take a chance.

The first four steps of this trick should be completed indoors.

1. Fasten a leash to your cat's harness. There is no need to remove the cat's collar; the harness will fit right over it.
2. While you keep your eye on the cat, so it doesn't get into trouble, have the animal drag the leash around, at least for brief periods, for two or three days.

3. Pick up the leash. Allow the cat to lead as you follow behind. If the cat tolerates this, proceed with the trick. Should the cat immediately lie down on its stomach, forget about this trick; review previously mastered tricks or learn a new one instead.

4. Once the cat seems adjusted to leading you, it's your turn to lead. Apply a little pressure to the leash. Tug softly and walk the cat. Give the animal plenty of time to adjust. With this trick, as with all the others, you are the best judge of when your cat is ready to advance to the next step.

5. Take the cat outdoors. Go for a short walk. This is not the way to stroll down Fifth Avenue in New York. Instead, opt for a nice quiet walk in your neighborhood or backyard. Plan to go no farther than a block or two. Walking on a leash in traffic is far more than most cats can handle.

My store is located in a shopping center. About one and a half blocks away is a small restaurant called the Summit. Sometimes I'll walk over there with one of the cats on a leash. The cat isn't allowed among the tables. But we stand together in the vestibule, making such a good conversation piece that I usually get a free cup of coffee.

Personalized Tricks

Now it's the cat's turn to train you—as if it hasn't already. Observe your cat carefully. See what it does naturally. Then add a bit of pizzazz and reinforce with a morsel of reward.

Tasha, for example, likes to jump up on my right shoulder. "Likes" is putting it mildly. She abhors my left shoulder and is adamant about jumping up only on the right one. I have no idea why and, believe me, this is

Tasha will jump
only onto my
right shoulder.

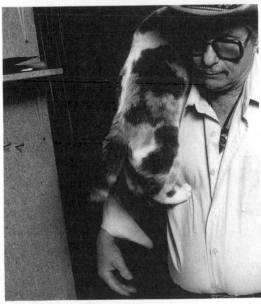

nothing I taught her. But she'll stand with her hind legs on the training table, her front paws against my chest. If I scoot her to my left side, she scoots herself to the right, then hops up. To tell you the truth, this would have been a very difficult routine to teach. But, being something of a ham myself, I've helped her make it a trick.

"Tasha won't do left shoulders," I announce. Sure enough, she jumps on my right shoulder. I move her to the left. She jumps to the right.

Undoubtedly, your cat has its own storehouse of idiosyncratic behaviors. To shape them into tricks, reinforce the actions with a treat. Does your cat knock off your hat? Dash through your legs? Kiss your cheek? Reward the cat. Offer praise.

Now you've both got some new tricks for the act.

6. Giving Cat Performances for Pleasure and Profit

Your cat is now able to perform. For many amateur trainers, this will be more than enough. Through the training process, your devotion to your cat has increased. Likewise, the cat cares more about you. In fact, the animal sometimes seems to obey you better than your children do. You are quite satisfied.

HOME PERFORMANCES

Still, you may enjoy further validation. Especially at first, training triumphs are best shared with relatives and good friends. Invite a select group to your home. Haul out the training table. Then, with as much hoopla as you can contrive, coax your cat through its routines. All along, the animal has received your nonstop praises. Now you're the one entitled to "Bravo!"

Remember, most people—even the most ardent cat lovers with the most pampered pets—do not believe that cats can do anything before audiences besides preening for judges. You and your trained pet will surprise them.

Still, your confidence may need additional massaging. Try another small group. If you have young children, consider performing at one of their birthday parties. But first, as objectively as possible, size up your animal. Is it of the right temperament for a houseful of lively, curious children? Earlier acclimatization to pot banging and lid clanging may pay off here.

At the birthday party, some youngsters will want only to play with the cat. If you're going to put your pet in this situation, make sure it's the kind of animal that will tolerate the sentiment.

At some shows I've done for children, particularly hospitalized children, the kids couldn't have cared less about sitting still to watch the tricks. Thrilled about the break in their routine, all they wanted was to cuddle the cats. On such occasions, I plan ahead, bringing only the most obliging troupe members. The Hisser, even though she has mellowed somewhat over the years, continues to live up to her name. She is never passed around at shows.

SENIOR CITIZEN GROUPS

In search of other potential audiences, don't forget senior citizen centers and nursing homes. Such facilities are almost always looking for performers. This will also give you the chance to polish your own patter and your getup. Being something of a lifelong country boy, I am most comfortable in cowboy boots and Western-style jeans and jacket. That's what I wear in my shop and on the road. Perhaps you would prefer something with a bit more glitz. Just keep in mind that anything you wear will be accessorized with cat hair.

NAMING YOUR SHOW

Pick a name for your act. Think in terms of something that will look good on a marquee, or at least in a Kiwanis club newsletter announcing your upcoming appearance. Because my troupe members have come and gone—I still miss Oscar terribly—I have stuck with "George Ney and His Performing Cats." Though fairly straightforward, this has in no way inhibited the alliterative and creative skills of the media. My "tricky menagerie" and "fine-tuned furry felines" have been singled out for being "the cat's meow." In one of my favorite descriptions, Miss Hiss was called "ornery but sultry."

TALKING IS IMPORTANT

In front of an audience, you'll need your own adjectives. Particularly if it's just you up there with one performing cat, you'll have plenty of time to talk. That's one reason I taught Tasha eighteen tricks. I needed to round out the act.

And don't forget to make a fuss over your cat as it performs. The cat has come to expect this. You already know the phrases. After using them at home during training sessions, they are as deeply engraved on your brain as on the cat's. Also, encourage audience participation. Select an assistant from the crowd. You'll have someone to talk to and to grab a cat, if necessary.

AVOIDING RUNAWAYS

Obedience training will theoretically keep your cat onstage or on the table during performances. But don't be too trusting. In general, you can trust a cat as far as you can reach, and that's it.

Whenever you travel outside your home for a show, place the animal in a carrier or cage. These are available at most pet shops. Cats need to roam; I'd be the last to argue for sequestering a pet. But transporting an animal to and from your vehicle is a different story.

The day I bought Madame Tanya in St. Louis, I carried her to the van in my arms. She was only four months old. I didn't want to frighten her. But my plans backfired. When a passing motorist blasted his horn, the Madame was so startled that she clawed and bit me, then wriggled out of my arms and under my van. To block her, six of us from the cat show dropped to our knees and extended our arms.

Poor Madame. Trembling, she cowered behind one of the van's tires. Had it been possible for her to vanish, never to face hands or horns again, I'm sure she would have. I shot my arms forward and grabbed Madame Tanya. As I held her, she was still quivering.

Inside the van, she avoided me. The whole way home, she hid under some cat furniture.

Sometimes I still blame that day for the fact that the Madame has never been as close to me as the other cats. At my store, she would hide, spending hours under my furniture. I don't know that she was ever happy. She was a good performer but, somehow, she never overcame that standoffishness.

When I retired her, she went to live with a friend of mine who has four other cats. In this household, she thrives. She sleeps on the bed and has the run of the place. No longer does she worry about being picked up, lugged off, and driven hundreds of miles to perform. I'm happy for the cat.

The friend she's living with, Susan Hochstadter, is the one who entered the Madame in the cat show where she won her ribbons. That day the Madame was in her glory. The judge simply judged her. No demands were made on her.

Cat House Originals
(*Brad Burt Photo, courtesy Rockford, Illinois,* Register Star)

Whenever I see the Madame, I get the feeling she dislikes me, strongly. She won't have anything to do with me. Months ago, I thought I'd bring her back for a performance. This was to be a special occasion. I introduced her as the cat that once appeared in a 9 Lives ad. The Madame hissed. During the "Cat Chorus Line," she snapped at the other cats in line. Afraid she would attack the troupe, I had to put her off to the side. She isn't used to my other cats anymore. To her, they're strangers.

Sometimes I wonder what would have happened if I had carried her out to the van that day in a carrier, instead of in my arms.

So no matter how young the kitten, use a carrying case. Outside, in the open, a cat in your arms may not be in your arms for long.

Inside my van, I always let the cats run free. Tasha loves the dashboard. So do some of the others. When we travel, I bring along water, cat food, and a litter box. Especially if I've also packed my cat furniture, the cats are content part of the time to curl up on a familiar object and doze.

If you find that you alone can't carry your cat and the cage, and whatever props you need, bring along a helper.

GETTING PUBLICITY

By this time, you and your cat are probably picking up notoriety. Increase the momentum. Spread the word among Scout leaders, at shopping malls, charitable organizations, hotels, country clubs, and recreation centers. Let it be known that you and the cat or cats are available. If agents aren't barking at your door, run a classified ad.

Also, depending on your commitment, paint the name of your act on the side of your van or car. I've gotten quite a few calls that way.

Remember, every booking adds to your track record and could enhance your reputation. If you're lucky, advance word of your performances will be carried in newspapers, in fliers, and maybe in on-the-air calendars on the radio. Keep track of every such mention your cat receives. Budding actors and actresses need scrapbooks and résumés. Get to work. All this will be invaluable if you want to go on and build your reputation up to the point of being able to book performances professionally and for a fee.

OUTDOOR PERFORMANCES

A word of caution: requests for outdoor performances may come your way. Consider them carefully. I've done some outdoor shows that came off without a hitch. Others left even me gasping.

The cats and I were invited to the grand opening of a

pet shop that handled my furniture. The festivities took place outdoors. I was complimenting myself on just how well the troupe was performing when, all of a sudden, Valentine bounded off the performance table and up a nearby tree.

Quickly I found an agile youngster to climb up after her. She started to scratch. Unwilling to sacrifice boy or pet, I grabbed a blanket. Then four of us, one on each corner, stood there like dauntless firemen, yelling to the boy to yank Valentine over to an area between the branches and let her go. It was flying feline. Fortunately, the cat came down on the blanket. The boy came down on his own. From then on, I have stationed one volunteer from the audience at each end of every outdoor performance stage.

At the start of your cat's career, you will probably be your own booking agent. Do what the professionals do. When you arrange for a performance, bring along all the publicity materials from your previous shows. Also, get some professional-quality photographs of your pet. If the animal has already been pictured in a newspaper, see if you can buy some of the prints from the paper. Otherwise, have some taken.

THE CAT-SHOW CIRCUIT

Now you're ready for the feline equivalent of Hollywood—command performances on the cat-show circuit.

If you've never been to a cat show, by all means attend one. It's an experience. The first time, leave your cat at home; this visit is purely for research. Soak up the atmosphere. If there are no cat shows in your town, there are bound to be some close by. To pin down the particulars, contact pet shop owners or veterinarians, or check local newspaper listings.

From fluffy, puffy, and shiny to naturally scrawny, most cat shows spotlight every conceivable breed of feline.

Even the names of show cats are mind-boggling. From Gettysburg, Pennsylvania, I met an Abe LinCoon—a Maine coon cat—that claimed direct bloodlines to Genghis Coon and Daniel Coon. At a show in Arlington, Virginia, I came across a Klasikat's Rainbo Connection from Salinas, California, and a heavenly little kitty from Phoenix, Arizona, named Windborne Guardian Angel.

Watching the discerning judges rate the thoroughbreds is an education in itself. And talk about pampered! There will be cats with bibs to catch the drool while they dine. Glamour cats will sprawl across white lace coverlets on miniature brass beds. At a sweltering show in the Midwest, when a hotel's air conditioner malfunctioned, one kitty sat regally on a velvet-covered ice bag, further comforted by a pint-size, battery-operated fan. Meanwhile, her flush-faced owner almost keeled over.

At cat shows, you'll also see the latest in cat-related products, from gourmet foods to pink velour slipcovers for litter boxes, rhinestone-studded collars, and potty seats.

CAT ASSOCIATIONS AND CLUBS

The way things work, many areas have cat clubs that are affiliated with the national and international cat organizations. These organizations include the Cat Fanciers' Association, American Cat Fanciers' Association, International Cat Association, American Cat Association, Cat Fanciers' Federation, and Canadian Cat Association.

It's the local clubs that sponsor the cat shows. For a captive audience and crowds numbering from hundreds to thousands, they can't be beat. The one thing most shows don't have is a trained cat that does tricks; that's where you can come in.

For a complete roster of shows, check *Cats* magazine, P.O. Box 37, Port Orange, Florida 32029. A smaller roster appears in *Cat Fancy* magazine, P.O. Box 2431, Boulder,

Colorado 80322. Cat magazines generally are not available at newsstands. If you don't already subscribe, you can usually find copies at the library or in your veterinarian's office.

To plot your cat-show strategy, find a show as close to home as possible. Why drive with your cat for three hundred miles when you might be able to drive thirty? Along with each show listing in the cat magazines, you will find the name, address, and telephone number of a cat club member. Contact this person. Send the cat's résumé. Enclose newspaper clippings of your appearances at such events as Boy Scout dinners, neighborhood festivals, or school programs. Also enclose photos. Mention that your trained cat is novel and newsworthy enough to generate advance publicity that will increase attendance and revenues at the cat show. Offer to contact the media: Trained cats make popular features.

Some show promoters will find your offer appealing. They'll be happy for you to do all you can. Just don't expect to be paid. On the cat-show circuit, you're still an unknown commodity.

But even if the promoters turn down your services as an advance man and don't offer you center stage, don't despair. Perhaps you can still exhibit your cat at the show by paying twenty-five to thirty-five dollars to rent a booth. This will give you a performance spot—a table among hundreds of exhibitors.

Various shows have regulations about "loose" cats. Most likely, you will be asked to bring your cat into the show hall in a cage or carrier. Follow all rules; in my case, I have finally been given permission to break them. Many shows now allow me to wheel my performing cats into the hall in a baby stroller. That permission often took longer in coming than the whole cat-training process did.

At the show, you will meet cat lovers. Show off your pet. Try to convince someone with cat-related products that your feline is an ideal model and attention-getter.

Then you can split the booth rental fee at an upcoming show—or, better yet, the other exhibitor can pay for all of it in exchange for your cat's ability to draw customers. Tasha started her career as a backdrop for my cat furniture.

Cat shows can pack hidden benefits. You never know who may be in the crowd. A number of times my cats have been hired for commercials simply because an agent, who happened to be at a cat show, remembered them.

Once you've done a show or two in your hometown, you're ready for an out-of-town cat show. Alert the newspapers and TV stations in the city where you're headed that you and your trained cat will be arriving. My approach with the media is to be something of a pest. If reporters are too busy, they'll tell you so. And if they're interested, you've got one story, which can lead to two more elsewhere.

With a performing cat, there are no guarantees that you will make a fortune. But then again, not all payoffs have to be financial. A trained cat is an endless source of pleasure, entertainment, and enough escapades to fill a book!

7. Making Your Cat Feel at Home

Suppose you're getting things together for a training session, and your cat jumps up on your lap and purrs. Or you're cutting out newspaper stories about your feline celebrity and there she is, right on your shoulder.

The cat is comfortable with you. She knows she can do no wrong. She's secure. Still, there are other ways in which you can help make her life comfortable and contented.

NEUTERING

For your cat, neutering is a must. Let's face it, anything alive is a sexual being. And particularly for a cat, operating as it does on instinct, there are times when mating is the only thing on its mind. For a performing cat, this presents special problems. You and your cat are all ready to do a trick when the animal catches the scent of another feline; forget about the trick and, at least temporarily, about your animal.

Moreover, neutered cats become more docile and people-oriented. The proper age at which to spay a female is about six months. With males, wait until eight to ten months.

LITTER TRAINING

Litter training does not have to be taught. With cats, it's instinctive. If you bring a new cat or kitten into the house, the most you should have to do is show it the litter box. Even in nature, felines normally paw a hole and bury their feces; this is one habit that dogs, despite their finesse as performers, would never think of initiating.

As innovations go, commercially packaged litter is fairly modern. It dates from the 1940s when a fellow removed some gravel from a pit, put it in sacks, and sold it at grocery stores.

More recently, it was decided in some quarters that naturally well-groomed, immaculate cats could be even more sophisticated. Some pet shops now handle kitty potty seats. There are slight variations, but basically the seat is a plastic device that fits over your own toilet seat. In the bottom of the kitty seat is a litter tray. To compel the cat to use the seat, other litter boxes are removed from the house. Once the cat learns to jump up and use the seat, your next step is permanently to remove the detachable litter tray from the bottom.

For a while there was talk of yet another refinement. This was to be a special device that fitted underneath the toilet seat and activated the toilet's flushing mechanism every time the cat jumped on and off. What next?

In all honesty, this is one brand of training I haven't tackled. My van has no plumbing.

SCRATCHING POSTS AND HOUSES

If you're worried about your cat scratching or otherwise marring your furniture, a scratching post could be a wise purchase. I hesitate mentioning this since I make scratching posts and houses and don't want this to sound like a commercial. Certainly, many brands are available. But by giving your cat its own belongings, you may preserve your own in the process.

Cats have pads on their paws that are like calluses on human hands. The pads can itch. Thus, the cats often like something to rub their paws against. Many people buy a scratching post or piece of cat furniture before their cat even arrives. Then you simply take the cat over and show it the furniture. If necessary, you can increase the appeal of the object by spritzing it with catnip spray; usually this is not necessary.

GIVE YOUR CAT AN ID TAG

What is necessary, however, is that identification tag for your cat's collar. One summer I was performing at the Strassenfest, a German festival in St. Louis. Fearful of running out of gas on the bridge on the way into the city, I stopped at a filling station in East St. Louis. Although I didn't know it at the time, municipal officials there had recently announced a new policy. To curb a string of slayings and robberies of out-of-towners stopped at traffic lights, the stoplights had been set just to flash red after 7:00 P.M. The aim was to prevent anyone from being unnecessarily detained in East St. Louis.

Unfortunately, Valentine had not consulted with municipal officials. When I got across the bridge and into St. Louis, I discovered that she was missing. Luckily, she was wearing an identification tag. The owner of the filling station immediately telephoned my shop in Illinois. Pausing only briefly for flashing lights, I retrieved Valentine.

She didn't say thank you. She never does. But then again, she didn't have to. Cats are like that. I know she loves me.

And I love her, too, as I do all my cats. From mere kitten love, our bonds have deepened. Relationships with cats are like relationships with people: from sharing frequently comes caring.

The cats and I have shared so much. Beyond the daily experiences that are part of having a cat in the family, we have shared training sessions, performances, and satisfaction.

When you educate your cat, and that cat responds to you and does tricks, something special happens. And it's worth all the time and all the effort that you've put into it.

Index

Age to start training, 40–41, 53
"All About Animals," 18–19,
    37–38
American Cat Association, 104
American Cat Fanciers' Associ-
    ation, 29, 104
American Veterinary Medical
    Association, National Pet
    Week, 22
Animal Consultants, 17
Associations, cat, 104–105
Attention span, 10, 38–39, 54, 81

Barrel, see Roll Out the Barrel
Baton, see Jump over the Baton
Beg, 11, 16
    teaching, 69–72

Behavior problems, 51
"Bozo Show," 14, 15
Breeds of cats, trainable, 37
Butkus, Dick, 22

Cages, 100, 102, 105
Canadian Cat Association, 104
Capital Cities Cable, 18
Carrying case, 100, 101, 105
Car travel, 43–45, 100–101
Cat-a-Back, see Play Dead
Cat Chorus, 35, 101
    teaching, 80–81
Cat Fanciers' Association, 104
Cat Fanciers' Federation, 104
Cat Fancy, 16, 22, 88, 104–105
Cat Fancy Almanac, The, 22

Cat House Originals, 26
Cat-show circuit, 103–104,
    105–106
Cats, 22, 104
Changes, cats adapting to,
    45–49
  different trainers, 47–49
  a new cat, 46–47
  a new family member, 45, 47
Clubs, cat, 104
Commercials, 22–24, 101,
    105–106
Countertops, jumping on, 51

Daniels, Mary, 40
Davis, Jim, 28
Death-Defying Trick, The, 16
  teaching, 68–69
Defecating outside the litter
    box, 47
  see also Litter box
Development, stage of, 49, 78,
    80
Discipline, 51
Drbal, Tom, 9, 22

Egyptians, 30
Electrical cords, chewing on,
    51
Expectations of your cat, 33–34

Failure, cat's sensitivity to, 52
Feeding, 47, 61, 64, 102
  see also Treats as rewards
Forgue, Dave, 18
Forgue, Joan, 18
Fowler, Jim, 19
Frequency of training sessions,
    39, 54
Furniture for cats, 2–9, 109

Garfield (cat), 28
"Gender preference" of cats, 45
"George Ney and His Perform-
    ing Cats," 22, 30, 99

Hall, Al, 14
Hallmark greeting cards, 12–14

High chair, eating in a, 14, 22,
    28, 52
  teaching Out to Dinner,
    81–84
Hochstadter, Elizabeth, 19, 20
Hochstadter, Karen, 19, 20
Hochstadter, Susan, 19, 20,
    100
Hodges, Mark, 18
Home performances, 97–98
Hoops, *see* Jump Through a
    Hoop
"How to Train Your Cat," 20

Identification tag, 109–10
International Cat Association,
    104

Jealousy among cats, 46–47, 50
Jumping barricades, 16
Jump over the Baton, 28
  teaching, 78–80
Jump Through a Hoop, 14, 19,
    22, 40, 49
  teaching, 75–78

Kittens:
  obedience training for, 41–42
  preparing, for training, 41–42
  stage of development, 49, 78

"Lady Blue," 24
Leash, Walking on a, 93–94
Length of training sessions,
    38–40, 54
Lie Down, 10, 22, 49
  teaching, 58–60
Litter box, 47, 102, 108
Love between cat and its
    owner, 33, 74, 97
  showing affection through
    touch, 36–37, 47
Luke, Bonnie, 6–7, 19, 20

Madame Tanya (cat), 19, 31, 46,
    74, 100–101
Mastery of a trick, 50, 57
Minorini, Reno, 18

Miss Hiss (cat), 15–17, 19, 31, 33, 46, 47, 50, 74, 86, 98, 99
Misty (cat), 25, 41

Naming your show, 99
New cat, old cat adapting to, 46–47
Neutering, 107–108
New family members, cat adjustment to, 45, 47
Ney, Cheryl, 25, 41
Ninske, Ray, 22
Noise toleration, 42–43, 54, 65

Obedience training, 41–42, 54–55
Operator, Please! (answering a telephone), 28
teaching, 84–85
Organizations, cat, 104–105
Oscar (cat), 3, 21–24, 46, 74
Outdoor performances, 102–103
Out to Dinner (eating in a high chair), 14, 22, 28, 52
teaching, 81–84

Peanut Butter (cat), 20–21, 24
Performances, 97–98, 99, 105–106
Perkins, Marlin, 19
Persian cats, 38
Personalized tricks, 94–96
Petting, see Touching your cat
Photographs of your cat, 103, 105
Piano, playing a toy, 14, 52
teaching, 88–89
Play Dead, 6, 14, 16, 17, 20, 22, 30, 38, 42
teaching, 64–68
Popowycz, Dr. Petro, 20
Praise, 10, 33, 42, 51–52, 55, 60, 65, 69, 73, 84, 86, 92, 96, 99
Publicity, 102, 105–106

Queen and Her Court, The, 16, 47, 48
teaching, 86

Repetition, importance of, 49
Rewards, see Praise; Treats as rewards
Riding in a baby stroller, see Strolling Those Babies
Roll Out the Barrel, 14
teaching, 90–93
Roll Over, 10–11, 16, 22, 30, 49
teaching, 60–64
Runaways, avoiding, 99–101

Schedule, training, 38–40
see also Time to learn tricks, amount of
Scottish Folds (breed), 7, 19, 20, 37
Scratching posts and houses, 109
Scupa (cat), 25–26, 28, 41, 43, 46, 47, 51, 65
Senior citizen groups, performing for, 11–12, 98–99
Shake Hands, 11
teaching, 71–74
Siamese cats, 37–38
Sit Down, 10, 16, 22, 30
teaching, 53–57
Sleeping patterns, 39–40
Snoop (cat), 9
Spooker (cat), 28–29, 80
Starting cat training, 32–55
age for, 40–41, 53
attention span, 38
building logically on previous tricks, 49
car travel, 43–45
choice of trainer, 45, 47–49, 53–54
discipline, 51
expectations of your cat, 33–34
knowing when a trick is mastered, 50, 57
length of training sessions, 38–40
noise toleration, 42–43, 54
obedience training, 41–42, 54–55

Starting cat training (*cont.*)
  on days and off days, 50–51
  one cat at a time, 50
  praise, 51–52, 55
  preparing kittens, 41–42
  repetition, importance of, 49
  stage of development and, 49
  touching, importance of,
    35–38, 41, 42, 52, 53, 55
  trainable breeds, 37–38
  training table, 34, 42, 54
Staying on training table, 42,
    49, 54–55
Strolling Those Babies, 14,
    21–22, 27, 28, 30
  teaching, 86–88

Table for training, *see* Training
  table
Talking to the audience, 99
Talking to your cat, *see* Praise
Tasha (cat), 7–15, 16–17, 19, 22,
    31, 33, 40, 45, 46, 47, 52,
    55, 60, 74, 88, 92–93, 94–96,
    99
  tricks learned by, 10–14
Tchaikovsky Tomcat (playing a
    toy piano), 14, 52
  teaching, 88–89
Telephone, answering a, 28
  teaching, 84–85
Time to learn tricks, amount of,
    10, 11, 14, 16, 21, 30, 40,
    55–57
  frequency of training
    sessions, 39, 54
  length of training sessions,
    38–40, 54
Toilet seat, kitty, 108
Touching your cat (petting), 42,
    52
  before training starts, 35–38,
    41, 53, 55
  training your cat and, 10, 34,
    60, 65, 92

Trainer, choice of, 45, 47–49,
    53–54
  substitute coaches, 47–49, 54
Training table, 34, 42, 54
  teaching cat to stay on, 42,
    49, 54–55
Travel, car, 43–45, 100–102
Treats as rewards, 11, 16, 19,
    40, 42, 52, 55, 61–64, 69,
    72, 77, 78, 81–84
  see also Feeding
Tricks, teaching, 53–96
  Beg, 69–72
  Cat Chorus, 80–81
  Death-Defying Trick, The,
    68–69
  Jump over a Baton, 78–80
  Jump Through a Hoop, 75–78
  Lie Down, 58–60
  Operator, Please!, 84–85
  Out to Dinner, 81–84
  Personalized, 94–96
  Play Dead, 64–68
  Queen and Her Court, 86
  Roll Out the Barrel, 90–93
  Roll Over, 60–64
  Shake Hands, 72–74
  Sit Down, 53–57
  Strolling Those Babies, 86–88
  Tchaikovsky Tomcat, 88–89
  Walking on a Leash, 93–94

Valentine (cat), 3, 20, 47, 50,
    60, 74, 103, 109–10
Victoria (cat), 26–28, 31, 42, 47

Water gun, 51
Whitney, Charlene, 26, 28, 45
"Wild Kingdom," 19

Yelling at your cat, 50, 51, 74

Zerr, Ed, 15, 48